DOWNLONG DAYS

DOWNLONG DAYS

A St. Ives Miscellany

A history of the lower part of the town known as
Downlong, from personal memory and previously
published works, chiefly The St. Ives Weekly Summary
and The Western Echo.

Eddie Murt
1994

Acknowledgements

My grateful thanks go to the St. Ives Museum Committee for the research facilities made available to me; to Mrs. Sylvia Rule for deciphering and changing my scribble into the English language, and to Tom Richards for putting the text on to word processor and preparing it for the printer, also his constructive comments and encouragement.

I am also indebted to Mr.A.Major, Mr.H.Noall, Mrs. S.Rule and Miss J.Stevens for the loan of their postcards to add to my own for the production of the illustrations.

E.M.

"DOWNLONG DAYS"
© Eleanor Murt
First Edition published June 1994
Typeset by Tom Richards and GBC Graphic Design & Print, 232 Wick Road, Brislington, Bristol BS4 4HN
Cover design by Toni Carver
Printed and published by
The St. Ives Printing & Publishing Company
High Street, St. Ives, Cornwall TR26 1RS

ISBN 0 948385 17 0

Cover photograph by Studio St. Ives: *Alfred Wallis's horse and cart in front of his premises on the Wharf.*

i

DEDICATED TO

The officers and men of HM Corvette *Allington Castle* for fishing a "Hake" from Arctic waters in 1945, thus enabling earlier days to be remembered.

Eddie Murt
1926 - 1993

Eddie was firstly a St. Ives man; a Cornishman who strongly upheld local traditions. He had a dry sense of humour that can only have come from a lifetime spent in Downlong as "one of we", and with fishing families, boats, crews, tides and fish.

As a writer he could describe a plate of "raw fry" so that you could taste the ingredients from the page as you read.

A kindly, practical, practising Christian who was first at the top of the ladder when the Chapel roof needed repair.

While he has gone to a better place, he leaves Downlong Days as part of his memorial to the Town he loved. His words and sentences contain the essence of St. Ives, so read his book carefully, because like life itself it is meant to be savoured.

H.L.

CONTENTS

CONTENTS (cont.)

CONTENTS (cont.)

Note: Extracts from The St.Ives Weekly Summary and The Western Echo are indicated by *SWS* and *WE* respectively.

PROLOGUE

The town of St. Ives

One of the finest single-handed sailing trips in history came about by accident. Hya, an Irish Princess, arrived on the Irish shore only to find that she had missed the boat; her Missionary friends had sailed. Like so many since, she had intended to come to Cornwall to change things. The fact that they had sailed was a disappointment, but imagine her joy when, by touching a leaf with her rod, it grew big enough for her to embark. With a smart bit of sailing and navigation she arrived in this Bay and picked her place to land before her friends arrived and landed in the surf on the eastern shore. All went well and she changed the people into Christians. They were so impressed that the community changed the name of the place to Porth Ia, Ia's cove, afterwards to St. Ie's and it later became St. Ives.

The town for many years had been divided into Uplong and Downlong. Whether this should be Upalong and Downalong is open to question. So too is the dividing line between the two districts. Some would say that Downlong is from the Market Place to the Island. On the other hand, people Downlong always regard going above Digey/Fore Street corner as going "up town", "upstreet" or "uplong", so it is for the reader to make up his own mind.

At the commencement of this narrative there was no Ayr housing estate with the "Tre" street names, and no Penbeagle estate, only fields, so the town then had no comparison with the size of the postwar town.

The chief occupation was with the sea and the many spin-off industries connected with the fishing industry. Every other man was a Captain. There were the Board of Trade ones, many certified in sail and steam. They lived on The Terrace and exercised on The Malakoff. The uncertified ones had skippered fishing boats under sail, and now with motors. They lived in the streets and passageways Downlong, and they walked back and forth in front of the Lodges. Then every boat had a Shore Cap'n who came ashore to let the younger men work. It could be said they practically lived in the net lofts, as they had no time to spare. Then there were a vast number of men who had reached the age when "Cap'n" was a mark of respect, or perhaps their nickname was more familiar than their true name, and it was better to give them a title than risk offending them. The next time you come to St. Ives on the seafront, and someone calls you "Cap'n", if you haven't got a boat or ever had one it's for you to decide which category you belong to.

1 THE DOMESTIC SCENE

Another "Hake"

I was born at No. 10 Fish Street, St. Ives, Cornwall in the February of 1926. As was the custom in those days, it is highly probable that my Mother had spent all of January in the house. It was usual to stay indoors for a month before the happy event.

The birth itself would be in the house, presided over by the midwife. If a Doctor was required someone would proceed to the surgery or the Doctor's house to pass on a message. Telephones were not for ordinary people.

Arrangements would have been made previously for a lady to come to the house to 'keep in' the new mother, who then spent a fortnight in bed, whilst all the housework and food preparation was done for her. Now instant return to household duties is the modern way. At that time most babies were born at home. This right of being born in the town of their forefathers has now been taken away from the children of the town. After a period of having Redruth "HAKES", we now have Penzance and Truro "HAKES", which is making the true St. Ives "HAKE" a rare specimen. In spite of all the changes that are forced on us, the one thing that cannot be removed is my birthright to call myself a "HAKE", which is an improvement on many other things I might have been.

It may be surprising to some that there should be any mention of hake, as no fish features on the coat of arms of the town. History has it that net fishermen of the town suffered much damage to nets and to fish already enmeshed, by attacks from the hakes which were then plentiful in these waters. As a warning of what was in store for them, one of their number was paraded around the town, at the same time being flogged by the fishermen. There is little doubt that it worked as the hakes disappeared, but unfortunately the herrings and pilchards must also have got wind of the affair, as they too disappeared. When in a leg-pulling mood our unenlightened neighbours still ask the question "Who flogged the Hake?".

Naturally there is little I recall of my first few years. It would be safe to say that life was slower and changes came slowly. Life in the town in the year of my birth was probably similar to that four years later when these memories begin. It would be fair to say that events and situations recorded are of the period from 1930 onward. They are typical of the life and times of boys living Downlong and would have been of little interest if not for the tremendous changes made during the last 60 years, accelerated by the war years and the changes in population which followed. These changes have completely altered the town and the inhabitants' way of life.

SWS February 1901   A LITTLE PARADISE
In discussing St. Ives in the Morning Leader recently, A.B.Walkley thinks the Artists Colony have lighted upon a little paradise. There is something foreign about the Cornish Folk, a strange tongue, a physical type which, whatever it may be, is certainly not the normal type of England. They strike me as peaceful enough, but it is said they can be very fierce upon occasion if you dwell with any emphasis upon the word "Hake".

Paternal and maternal

As soon as I was old enough to understand, it became obvious that I had been born into a seafaring family, as were the majority of the Downlong community.

At this time Father was fishing in the *Sheerness,* this being one of the larger boats and a "hard shutter". She was often at sea when the rest of the fleet were in harbour. Starting his life as a Telegram Boy, Father moved on to learn his trade as a shoemaker with Mr. Bob Chard. With the good money being earned by herring fishing during the First World War, and a widowed mother with four youngsters to rear, his apprenticeship didn't last long. Grandmother had an allowance from the "Pendeen

Distress Fund" of five shillings per week and two shillings for each child until the age of 14.

Almost every house had seafaring connections. The majority of men were fishermen, but many also had other sea-going activities. Many men went "steamboat sailing", making a trip in one of Hain's steamships between seasons, or in coastal vessels known as "weekly boats", trading to Hayle with coal for the power station, but always with the intention of returning to St.Ives in time for the winter herring season.

Other men went yachting in the summer months, spending their time at Cowes or Monte Carlo, again getting home for the herring season. A number of men were members of the Royal Naval Reserve and went away to do their drill every year, joining not out of patriotism, but to help to pay the rates.

Every man was involved with the Lifeboat service, either as crew members or launchers when required. At this time the crew numbered 15 men, and a great number of men were required to pull the boat and carriage to the water's edge.

Having had very bad eyesight from boyhood, Father had been turned down for Naval service, but had some service in the local lifeboat. His first service was on the 10th October 1917 when, with the majority of the crew being first timers, they went to the steamer *Sea Point*. Whilst alongside, the lifeboat's mast went up through the ship's lifeboat which had been swung out on the steamer's davits. After chopping away the mast, they then rescued the crew of 15. On a later occasion whilst seated in the boat, Father was asked to vacate his position as it was expected to be a difficult trip and the wearing of spectacles would be an impediment. On being replaced by a relative of the Coxswain he ceased his connection with the lifeboat's activities.

With regard to the sea connections on my Father's side, these concerned the Murts and the Rowes. Grandfather Murt, besides fishing had sailed on the local vessel

Elwood. On Boxing Day 1908 he was a member of the crew of the *Pendeen* owned and skippered by Tommy Rowe, a brother of my Grandmother. Together with the *Doris* they sailed for Bassett's Bay, but only the *Doris* returned. That night my Grandmother lost her husband and her brother. At the first opportunity the *James Stevens No. 10* searched the area but found nothing. Grandmother's brother Charlie Rowe had his first lifeboat trip that day. He was later to become the Harbourmaster at St.Ives after being a survivor of the sinking by a U-boat of the Portreath steamer *Olivia* during the First World War.

In November 1927 tragedy again came close when the *Day Dawn* struck the Stones reef, and Tommy Rowe, the son of the skipper of the *Pendeen* was one of the three survivors of the crew of five who were picked up by his uncle's boat the *Godrevy*.

My Mother was also from two fishing families. On her father's side, the Peters, and on her mother's side, the Eddy's. She herself had served her time as a tailoress at Simpsons in Fore Street, and had never ceased to sew all her life. On her mother's side there had been losses at sea also. On May 7th 1884 the lugger *Brothers* was taken aback in a squall and sank when sailing home from the mackerel ground. Richard Eddy aged 15 years and William, my Grandmother's brothers, were drowned with the other three men, William Eddy's father-in-law and brother-in-law being two of them.

During the First World War there was a near tragedy which had a happy ending. On 8th February 1917 the lugger *Mary Ann* skippered by Mr. Matthew Stevens Senior, was sunk by a bomb placed in her by a U-boat crew in their campaign of total destruction. The crew were allowed to climb into their punt and were left to their fate until picked up by a passing steamer. In the crew were Mr. James Eddy, Grandmother's brother; Mr. Matthew Stevens Senior, her brother-in-law, and Mr. Stevens Junior, her nephew.

In September 1919 the Hain steamer *Treveal* set out

from Cardiff bound for Port Said with bunker coal. From Port Said she went on to Calcutta and in January 1920 was on her way from Calcutta to Dundee with jute and manganese ore when she went ashore at Kimmeridge Ledges on the Dorset coast. Of the seven St. Ives men lost that night one was James Bassett, the son of my Grandmother's sister, Eliza Annie. The wages due to James Bassett for this voyage amounted to £38.5s.7d but the following is a copy of a statement received by his mother from the owners:-

Expenses incurred on behalf of James Bassett, sailor, drowned 10/1/20, for which the owners are not liable.

R.Bartlett bringing corpse from
beach and preparing grave for burial
at Worth Matravers.   15. 6.

J.Smith, coffin & fittings and
bringing corpse from Worth to Swanage.   £8. 15. 0.

L & SW Railway carriage corpse
Swanage to St. Ives Cornwall   £17. 17. 0.
                                                             £27. 7. 6.
                    Balance wages due £10. 18. 1.

On my mother's father's side the Peters seemed to have fared better in keeping their heads above water. My Grandfather Peters, with five of his brothers, were members of the Royal Naval Reserve who lined up at the St. Ives railway station on the call to the colours with the outbreak of the First World War. They all returned safely, but it is recalled that James Peters Senior laid up his boat at Lelant and came home and died of a broken heart. The Peters family until recent days have always maintained a connection with the local lifeboat activities.

The above tragedies were in no way confined to my family. Every house Downlong had similar or even worse stories to tell. They were the risks taken to provide food for the table and clothes for the backs of the children.

The language and sayings of the people Downlong, although the same as those used by people in the rest of the town, would present some problems to those across the Tamar, and in some cases to those much nearer the town. No doubt some words were handed down from the Cornish language, or words brought home from foreign trips. Others were nautical and many were from the tin industry.

In this narrative I have tried to refrain from using words which are unfamiliar to many readers, but are still used in the fishermen's Lodges, where the members are almost 100% "St. Ives men", which is quite different from "Men of St. Ives". I have also refrained from using nicknames, except in one case where "Man Friday" is mentioned. This no doubt removes much of the colour from the book, but it would possibly cause offence to some families to mention these names, although it was almost impossible to tell any story or carry on any conversation without the use of a nickname to distinguish one person from another of similar name. In fact some people answered to their nickname to the exclusion of their own. On the other hand, the nickname dare not be mentioned in front of others, but every family had a nickname which had been picked up from some careless remark or physical peculiarity. Some names would be difficult to spell and wouldn't look very nice in print.

In such an environment no doubt I would have heard my first words which doubtless was the question as to whether I was 'a boy or a cheeld'. Apart from the initial question, and regardless of sex, I would then have been referred to as 'the cheeld' for the rest of my childhood. This word was also used in other Celtic regions.

A few words in common use, rarely used today, concerning the Cornish coal fired cooking range which was in every house, are *Slab, Billis, Cherks, Creaved, and Shining like Dagwell,* which was the condition of the range when the black lead had been applied.

With regard to the meal table, there was *Raw fry, Rooty,*

Maws and *Grushens*. In the house there was a *Boot jack*, *Skeeter* and *Flasket*. The fishing conversation covered *Shoving in or out, Mollicks, Shangs, Shales, Reps* and a *Wink*, hopefully with a few *Gurries* as well.

The clock had *Flies*, and the shopping was done with a *Frail*. On cold days fingers had the *Gwenders*, eyes often had a *Wilk*, and sick people were described as *Wisht*.

The floor boards were the *Planchon*, the door was often of the *Epps* variety, the roof had a *Riffle* and the *Launder* leaked. To hurry along was to *Jail*, and often the room was like *Tommy Tribe's Bay. Emmets* were insects, as were *Grammersows*. The *Dumble Dory* kept to the Island, the *Mulley* to the pools, together with the *Normans* and the *Whistle fish*.

On the harbour front one might meet a *Bay man*, a man in a *Barwell*, or a woman in a *Soggett*. In the harbour a *Kidda* and a *Policeman* gull on the sand picking over pieces of *Balsh* among the *Ore- weed* on the tide mark.

At close of day it was up over the *Chamber stairs* with a candlestick, and be careful with the *Grace* and go to sleep quickly before *Jan Dark* comes to get you.

Home

Many of the houses Downlong are intertwined with one another. In describing one house, the same details would cover many others. Our house was at the top of a flight of stone steps, the cellar underneath being shared with a neighbour. This was used for storing coal, fishing nets, the washing and was sometimes used for drying the weekly wash, and had no partition of any sort.

The first floor consisted of a large room which had a partition. This formed a small room which rejoiced under the name of a back kitchen. It was pitch dark except in daytime when the front door was open, or a light was taken in. There was a small table on which stood a Primus stove; on the floor stood a bucket for all the liquid waste from the kitchen and this was emptied down the closet pan which was across the porch outside.

The large room had a Cornish range, always referred to as the "slab". This was the living room for all daytime uses. There was a big wooden table with kitchen chairs, with a couch taking up one side of the room. On the wall there was a pendulum clock with a horse standing on the top. A large picture of a woman clinging to the foot of a stone cross with the sea breaking at her feet, entitled "Rock of Ages", was hung on the wall. Almost every house had a biblical type picture, usually "The Woman at the Well", "Moses viewing the promised land" or "Daniel in the lion's den". A large oil lamp with funnel and globe to give light at night stood on the sideboard and was cleaned with newspaper every day. On the floor were straw and rope mats to cover the canvas, also pieces of sailcloth to protect the mats from wear and tear. The one window gave a view of passing traffic in Fish Street.

Climbing the wooden stairs we find the bedroom, where space is at a premium. Two beds, a wardrobe and dressing table take all the room. From the window at the front a view of roofs across the road; from the back window also a view of roofs, but in the distance Clodgy Point could be seen, and, by looking down, there was often a pony to be seen either in a yard or looking over the Epps door of the stable below.

As there was no electricity or gas there were no labour saving devices, and everything was done by hand with the exception of a treadle sewing machine. The walls of the rooms were papered and most of the woodwork was grained with dark stain, lime being used for whitening the ceiling.

Pull-down roller blinds covered most of the windows, with net curtains covering the bottom halves. A heavy oil-cloth covered the table at mealtimes and in the summer a sticky fly-paper hung from a beam to catch the numerous flies that came in.

There was no water supply indoors. The outside tap was

shared with a neighbour and an earthenware jug was always filled at night to supplement the iron kettles on the slab.

The key to the door was a large one and was only used at night, there being no need to lock the door if going out during the day.

Such were the conditions Downlong in which large and healthy families were born and raised, and except for the number of rooms it was pretty much the same in every house.

Although most families were attached to one or other of the Chapels and would probably not admit to any superstition, almost every house had a copy of *Old Moore's Almanack*. Whether this was out of pity for the person who came to the door selling them, or out of curiosity for the future, is not clear.

On the advent of lightning all mirrors were turned to face the wall or covered by a cloth. In spite of much enquiry the reason for this has been lost as it is not done today.

Although the bedroom ceiling was plastered and refreshed with lime when necessary, the other ceiling was open-beamed. The planchon was stained and five or six planks cut to form a trap hatch through which to move large items of furniture, and in many cases used to remove the occupants, complete with box, on their last earthly journey.

Almost every home also had a cat which helped to keep the mice away; with nets being repaired in the houses it was important that there should be no vermin to cause more damage. There were very few pet dogs. A cat in one house often had the fault for driving mice next door, so almost everyone had a cat.

Whilst my generation was just too late to have wild birds as part of the diet, wild birds were still caught, and in addition to the canary the finch and linnet were popular cage birds.

With the increase or decrease of the size of the family

moves were very frequent from one unfurnished accommodation to another. Very few people at that time owned their house. Mortgages had not reached this far west. On receiving the key of the new house it was then scrubbed thoroughly and after shifting the furniture on wheelbarrow or cart the old house was then scrubbed through before the key was given up. Since the war this seems to have changed, as I have seen new tenants' furniture passing the old ones on the stairs, and enough rubbish left behind to fill a lorry, which says much for the speed at which people now have to live.

Whilst it is deplored by many that so many houses Downlong are owned as a business proposition by people living away from the town, it would seem that 90% of Downlong at one time was owned by only a few people, as the item of sale below indicates, but then all houses were for rental.

NOTICE. At the Public Hall, St. Ives, on Monday and Tuesday 29th and 30th September 1919, sale of freehold lands and houses, property of Earl Cowley's Estates, comprising 21 smallholdings, building land, 139 houses and cottages, in the Borough and Parish of St. Ives.

Those on the outskirts of the town included cow and fodder house and stable, and other buildings, in some cases dwelling houses. These were at Stratton Vow, Nanjivey, Hellesvean, Carnello, Chy-an-Dour, Venton Vision, Pedn-na-Vounder, Higher and Lower Burthallan, Carrick Dhu, Rose Vale, Ayr [near St.Ives town], former engine house in Ayr field and freehold land at Treloyhan Downs.

With regard to houses at the Warren, it would seem there were very few that did not belong to Earl Cowley. Those for sale numbered 23. Rents per year, paid quarterly, varied from two shillings and sixpence to £9. The most common were £5 or £6.

Westcotts Court, Skidden Hill, St. Andrews Street, Street- an- Pol, accounted for 211 more lots for the sale.

The Terrace hadn't escaped the Earl, No 1 with Post

Office, 4, 7, 9, 13 and 19, and No.1 Albert Place, with low rents of around £1.8s. a year, but no doubt the rates were quite high.

Houses in the Digey came to six, Porthmeor Square four, Norway Square and Norway Lane, Back Road West six, North Place five, also the net manufacturing lofts in the occupation of Messrs. England & Son. Scores of lofts and studios too numerous to identify, but the names of the occupants were the backbone of the local fishing industry.

Thirteen houses in Porthmeor Road, in addition to studios and lofts, twelve houses in St. Peters Street, two in St. Lukes Court, only three in Fish Street, but he made up for it with a coal store as well as fish cellars and lofts. In Pudding Bag Lane he owned four cellars, two lofts, a salt house, and two cottages with entrances in St. Lukes Court. The Ropewalk hadn't escaped with seven lofts, a studio and a cellar in addition to cellars, lofts, press lofts, smoke house, salt house in the occupation of Mr. Whittaker the Fish Merchant.

The announcement of this sale must have been a great worry to the fishing community, although on studying the names it would seem that many occupiers were able to purchase their dwellings, lofts, studios, bakehouse and coal yard.

It would appear that Earl Cowley's favourite game was Monopoly. He missed out only on the railway station and waterworks, unless he was saving them for a later sale. In 1906 he had already sold the Island to the town for the sum of £650.

Washday

Monday was washday. It was done regardless of weather and a full day's work it used to be. We must remember there was no piped water, sink or drainage in the house. Water would have to be boiled either on the slab or in some cases in a little copper in the cellar with a coal fire underneath. A lot of the clothes had been soaking throughout the night in galvanised baths or wooden troys. The washing, on brass wash boards with soap and scrubber, according to the type of garment, was followed by rinsing the whites in clean water with blueing added. When deemed ready, everything went through the wooden rollers of the iron mangle. Those who had cellars did their washing there, but not everyone was so fortunate. Finally the water was tipped into the gutter or down the closet pan, whichever was the most convenient. The house would have been a cloud of steam and no place for the casual caller during this period. The caller would be welcome though to help carry the flasket of washing to the drying ground.

Depending on where you lived and the weather prospects the clothes were taken to the drying ground. For those near the Island the front slope was popular; to those nearer the Meadow the field where the Meadow Flats now stand and then known as the Barnoon field was used. This was very steep but suitable. If the sea was out the Porthmeor blue bowlie stones were soon covered, each item having a stone placed on the corner to keep them in place, and often the flasket left upturned by the side. In the harbour clothes lines were tied to suitable points. With a wooden prop held in position by a stone and hook formerly used as a pressing stone, the washing would then fly like flags in the wind. Others would hang a line between suitable nails or downpipes, and with a small prop would dry the washing against their own houses. If the day was wet the clothes were hung in the cellar until dry or the fine weather returned.

The great thing was that wherever the washing was put there it would stay, nothing would be stolen, and if it came on to rain a neighbour would look after it. One wonders what would happen to the clothing if put on the Island in this present age.

If drying had been completed the evening would then be taken up with ironing. The wedge shaped irons would be heated in the slab and transferred into the ironing box with a poker, another iron taking its place for a refill as soon as the first iron cooled. This was the main method of ironing until gas irons and those heated with a chemical block came on the scene. All were replaced with the electric iron as electricity became available.

Meals

With the exception of the times when it was necessary to have an early meal, 12 o'clock was dinner time and 4 o'clock was always tea time. Men would leave their work in the loft, or on the boat, knowing that the meal would be ready at those times.

Although salt herrings and boiled potatoes had by this time become less common as the staple diet, most houses had a "bussa" of herring and probably of butter as well. Beef, cabbage and potatoes were the usual Sunday dinner. Tripe and cowheel was a common meat dish. Rabbits were more common than now, but poultry was only for Christmas, the type of bird depending on the amount of herring caught. Raw fry, stew, pasty or broth was the weekday dinner. Fish was eaten in its season, as were cold slices of ling or cod roe. Marinated pilchards would last for most of the day. Chips were mainly home made.

Saturday was baking day for "heavy" cake, saffron cake and buns. Pasties were usually mid-week, each one made to the liking of the eater, with or without rooty, onion or whatever, each one marked and initialled to ensure people got the correct one, as they were lying on or overhanging the plate. A pasty was always eaten on its own, never with chips, as sometimes certain people do today.

Most houses had a string of onions bought from the French onion seller, who came to the door with strings of onions on a pole, parking his bike festooned with onions at a strategic position in the street.

Most houses had a nail outside on which a ray could be hung to dry before eating. Potatoes and apples were bought by the gallon, often from the carts which came around the streets. Foodstuff which might go off was salt-ed, and milk was boiled the same day as there were no

15

refrigerators and no-one could afford to throw food away. Food that had to be taken to sea was packed into a canvas bag known as a frail, or in a biscuit or sweet tin, held together with rope lashing. Butter was packed into a glass jar, and a loaf of bread was cut as required. Tea and condensed milk were already on board the boat. Any food not eaten was brought back home and eaten. No matter how short its stay aboard it always tasted "boaty" and no matter how it was disguised it was vile.

Blackberry tart was a treat for Sunday tea. Cream was only sixpence a quarter although very few could rise to this. Most families picked their own fruit or bought it from Willie Cattran who came around selling from a basket. The first pint of blackberries picked often made a news item in the Western Echo.

As if there was not enough fish about, dry fish - Newfoundland cod - was often bought from grocers and soaked all night in water before being eaten.

Until the wreck of the *Bessemer City* in 1936 there was not a lot of tinned fruit for Sunday tea. Prunes were usually eaten for tea with custard rather than for breakfast, but for quite a while after November 1936 sliced peaches or half pears were usually available, depending on the number of tins one was able to salvage and whether the label was intact. Tins from the same source also improved the tea table with red middle cut salmon, and in some cases families lived off this for many years.

WE August 1923   Mr. Samuel Allen of St. Eia Street, picked a large bunch of blackberries at Towednack on Thursday. We believe these to be the first gathered in this district for the season.

WE July 1933   On Monday a handful of splendid blackberries were picked. My friend told me that he has twice in recent years known blackberries to be picked on the 25th July. This year the record was broken by a day.

Cures

With the majority of fishing families not being able to afford Doctors' charges, most families put great dependence on herbs, with the Black Elder flower being the top of the list. After being picked it was spread out to dry, later to be hung on a nail outside the house before being put away in a paper bag for future use.

No slab was complete without an iron saucepan with elder flower steeping away, ready to be used for any ailment which might occur in the family. A "wilk" on the eye lid was bathed in it, temperature was brought down by drinking it, colds, coughs and almost any ailment were treated by drinking a cupful of it, sometimes made more palatable by the addition of a piece of liquorice ball which could be bought at the chemist.

With prevention being better than cure, many young children wore little bags of camphor round their neck to ward off colds. Others had Simpson's iodised lockets which were made from seaweed, for the same purpose.

Children suffering from whooping cough were taken to the gas works to breathe in the fumes from the retorts, which was supposed to assist the breathing.

Boils on any part of the body were treated with hot bread poultices to draw them out. Fishermen suffered from sea boils around the wrist caused by the chafing of the sleeve of the oilskin frock, and were aggravated each night, especially during the herring season. Any suggested cure was tried, but with very little success.

The daily callers

As a child the first regular visitors I can remember coming to the house were the roundsmen. The milkman should have called first, but, for some reason, ours often came in the evening, the milk being brought to the door in a pitcher and measured into a jug. The milk was boiled almost at once to keep it fresh.

The newspaper was delivered by the paper boy,

although he seemed to be a man to me. We used to have The News Chronicle or the Daily Herald. On the front of the paper there was a serial number which used to be cut out and pasted onto a card, which was proof of purchase towards the book that was on offer by the paper at a reduced price. The main paper was always The Western Echo. This was the Downlong paper. The most useful piece of news was the tide table and this was diligently cut out and put in a safe place in a tobacco tin, or inside the cap lining, as this was essential for the next week's working. Most children used to read comics. I used to have the Sunbeam, later changing to the Hotspur as reading tastes improved. At Christmas the newsagents gave away a calendar and this was another item found hanging on the wall inside most houses Downlong.

The Co-op bread roundsman was another regular, his basket covered with a green baize cloth and containing loaves of all shapes. On completion of payment a ticket with the "Divi" number was issued. The groceries from the Co-op were delivered on Saturdays, and for children lucky enough to visit the Co-op there was always the wonder of the wire which carried the money to the cash desk and later brought back the change and the receipt in the cup to the counter assistant. With the money due back from the "Divi" articles of clothing or footwear were picked up from the Penzance shop.

The most regular caller to the houses Downlong was Dr. Matthew doing his evening rounds, dressed in a long heavy mackintosh, gauntlet gloves and a trilby hat, riding a Sunbeam motor bike. On seven nights of the week it was possible to check one's clock by the time of his passing. If he was late it would be commented on, and if the bike stopped anywhere near, doors would open to see where the doctor was visiting in case assistance was required. Dr. Matthew was always received with respect, almost with reverence, his instructions in the same category as divine writ. Being an age when medicine was more fashionable than pills, his "mixture as before" was drunk in complete faith of a recovery. Extreme poverty made the payment of the doctor's bill rather a worrying experience. Whether the words attributed to him that "the people on the Terrace will pay" were ever uttered by him is debatable, but he was alleged to have passed on being owed many outstanding accounts. At the age of five, whilst sitting on my mother's lap at the Edward Hain hospital, I had my tonsils removed by Dr. Matthew. I was allowed home the same evening.

When the doctor's son came into the practice, he was always referred to as Dr. Pat, no doubt until he had proved his worth, and there was to be no question of confusion as to which Dr. Matthew was expected to call. A visit from the doctor often entailed a visit to the surgery in the Market Place to collect a bottle of medicine. There being no light except during surgery hours, a box of matches was essential for finding the bottles. One then had to search through the bottles, holding a match at the same time. Fortunately no fires ever resulted.

Island Road school

Those children living in the area between the Digey and Smeaton's Pier had their first schooling at this little school beside the Island gate. The tolling of the school bell was one of the familiar sounds of Downlong, and a reminder to the children in the area that the time had arrived for them to start their schooling with Mrs. Williams or Miss Sisley. I can only remember that we used to write with chalk on slates. During the afternoons we used to have a period when we folded arms and had a sleep.

The playground was very exposed to the winter winds. Mothers would bring hot drinks to pass through the school gate. They also went up on the slope overlooking the playground to watch the children at play. As we were only four and five year olds we were brought and fetched, so mothers must have had a busy time with housework and also during the herring season counting fish on the harbour front.

In school we saw our first bottled milk, a third of a pint bottle with a cardboard top and a press hole for the straw. The straws were real and not paper substitutes. In the winter the crates of milk were stacked around the Bogey coal fire which heated the classroom.

The caretaker at this time was Janie Stevens, who took over the duties from her mother. From the time of the school opening in 1896 and its closure in World War Two there had only been two caretakers.

SWS December 1899   A report on the school shows the children engaged in many interesting occupations, including fan drill, musical bell drill, marching, singing, reciting etc. this accounts for the high attendance.

WE 1940   The 7th June 1940 saw the closing of the school and its 53 children were transferred to the Stennack School on the opening of the new Belyars School on 17th June 1940.

The school was used at odd times by children evacuated during the war years, but on the occasion of the bombing of St. Ives gas works on 28th August 1942 and the loss of all gas in the town, it was opened for five weeks as an emergency cooking centre with electric cookers for those who had no other means of cooking.

The St. Ives Youth Club have been in occupation almost since the end of hostilities.

2 THE SOCIAL SCENE

Shops

Almost every street Downlong had a shop which opened all the year round. They were open for six days a week, and many, being part of the house, were not restricted to shop hours. Often these places were run by widows, or people who would find it difficult to earn a living any other way.

Starting from the entrance to the Meadow, Mr. Baughan ran a grocery shop where we used to buy vinegar and sticky flycatchers. In the Digey Mrs. Beckerleg sold paraffin. Back Road West had three grocery shops; Mrs. Payne, Mr. Freeman and Mr. Toman. In Mariners Square Mrs. Stevens sold herbie beer and paraffin. The Island Square was where Mrs. Ninnes sold wool, and opposite, Mr. Uren's shop in Island Road sold milk as well as sweets and groceries. In Fish Street there was a cobbler and a butcher. Mr. Wedge in Pier View and Mr. Couch in St. Eia Street sold groceries, whilst Mrs. Tanner in Burrow Road sold greengroceries and paraffin.

At the bottom of Bethesda Hill Mr. Cothey, and Mr. Laity at the bottom of Fish Street sold groceries, the latter specialising in tea. Mr. Herbert had a grocery at the bottom of Bailey's Lane, while at the bottom of Bunkers Hill Mr. Stevens met all the needs of the smokers. A few yards up Fore Street Mrs. Johns served groceries opposite Mr. Perkin's sweet shop, where a halfpenny would buy five sweets or a sherbet fountain. If the needs were not met there the next sweet shop was opposite Zion Chapel in "Small Martins" which distinguished it from Martins the Drapers, now replaced by Woolworth's store.

There were plenty of bakehouses about. Mr. Stoneman and Mr. Ward had theirs up a little lane opposite Fore Street Chapel, known as Flamanks Court. Mr. Trevorrow was in Hicks Court, and Mr. Thomas the Pasty King was in St. Peters Street. Mr. Trevorrow was at the top of Fish Street in Back Road East, whilst Mr. Smith was at Sea View Place. Mr. Dick Stevens at Carncrows Street and Mr. George Wedge at Pier View made bread and cakes, which were baked in the bakehouses.

Many people took trays of saffron buns, heavy cake, bread and other bulk baking to the public bakehouses.

Some householders sold marinated pilchards - "Mallios" - which were ordered the day before by taking a dish with a note regarding who owned the dish and the number of fish required. The fish spent the night in the bakehouse and were collected the next day. This trade was usually done when pilchards were being caught in Mounts Bay.

During the herring season kippers were sold from a house at the top of Fish Street, and were sold around the streets at twopence a pair.

There were also three fish and chip shops Downlong, Mr. James opposite St. Peters Street chapel, Mr. Wallace at Chy-an-Chy, and Mr. Long in Fore Street.

If a haircut or shave was required, the barbers shops were the great meeting places where time was of no importance. Mr. Barber was in Island Square, Mr. Thomas behind Dobles Wall and Mr. Toman in Fore Street, near the Digey.

There was very little need for anyone to go above Digey corner to do any shopping except perhaps to visit an iron-monger's shop. Everything that was needed was on sale in the Downlong area of the town. The Fishermens' Co-op on Wharf Road sold paint, rope, scrubbers and soap pow-der, but the most important thing for boys was fish hooks.

As there were no houses with electricity and not every-one had gas, there was a great demand for paraffin for lighting, so many shops sold this fuel in addition to every-thing else they sold.

Most of the shops further up the town had delivery boys with bikes or two-wheeled trucks. Shoe shops sent shoes on approval, usually four shoe boxes tied in a cloth. This was often done at times of bereavement, when the widow needed black shoes, but was never seen in the town until after the funeral.

No doubt I have omitted some shops from this list or perhaps the names of the owners have changed, but it will give some idea of the number of useful shops in almost every street.

Dustcarts

The regular callers at every house were the dustmen. There were no bins as today and the rubbish was either in a bucket or an old drum with the top cut out and a wire handle fitted. Most of the rubbish was fine ash as there were few tins, and anything that would burn was put on the fire. None of the buckets had lids, which added to the mess when the boys carried out their pranks of capsizing dust buckets on the way to school.

The rubbish was tipped into a horsedrawn cart which had long handled shovels and hooks hanging at the back, and with these the men also cleared the drains on their route. All the rubbish was taken to the dump on the Island. This was an iron pipe beside the Coastguard lookout, which was called the "Shute". All floatable objects went away on the tide, and very little ever came on to the beaches. There were lots of rats at the dump, and as boys we used to throw stones at them, some using air-rifles, which was an improvement on former generations who favoured a baited hook.

In 1890 a letter to The St. Ives Weekly Summary complained of *"... the smell of putrifying stuff at Trenwith Bal floors, which was town property. If the Board School was to escape an epidemic it would be no thanks to the town. In a town of 6,000 more than two scavengers were required, the town being at present without a Nuisance Inspector and the town reeks with odours...".* In 1899 there were complaints of *"...rubbish being thrown in the streets, to be removed by the sweepers, whereas it should be kept for the refuse collecting cart which readily visits all accessible parts of the town...*".

Confusion was being caused in March 1919 by the action of Capt. Short in railing off the dumping ground at Wheal Dream. He had not received the £1 per year as agreed with the Council. As a result of this the Council were asked to find a new dumping ground.

In the Borough Surveyor's report of 1920 we find that *"...the scavenging of house rubbish is effected thrice weekly. The scavengers work also embraces the cleaning of street gullies, but in spite of this the practice of dumping domestic rubbish on the harbour foreshore needs to be rigorously checked...".*

In spite of the Council search for a new dumping ground the Mayor reported in 1921 that as a result of an interview with Mr. J.T.Short, an agreement had been made for the dumping of all rubbish at Wheal Dream at a yearly payment of £5, all refuse to be dumped directly into the sea.

In 1925 the Council were again looking for a dumping site. This time the Committee visited two sites on the Island. They selected a site on the south east corner of the Old Battery, instructing the Surveyor to prepare plans and estimates for a concrete shute to facilitate immediate disposal into the sea.

Tenders were received in December 1925 for collecting house rubbish and street scavenging for 12 months from 31st January 1926. These were: Phillips Bros £659.9s., Craze Bros £640, W.S.Phillips £666.2s., Ben Phillips £624. Mr. Ben Phillips' tender was accepted.

Porthgwidden beach was receiving more than its fair share of rubbish in May 1927. Alderman Hollow drew attention to the fact that 20 loads of rubbish had been dumped by Corporation employed carts on that day. This was in spite of the shute at the Island being used as an experiment for one month during the year. An iron cylindrical shute was constructed in 1929.

The Island became the regular dumping ground from this date. In November 1936 the Council considered the possible use of the cliffs at "Horse's leap", but within days of the meeting the *Bessemer City* was wrecked in the vicinity and the amount of tinned fruit and other cargo which came up with the tide and grounded on Porthmeor beach was a strong argument for those opposed to this move.

In February 1937 the Council decided to seek a loan for the purchase of an incinerator, to be installed at Balnoon, Halsetown, but the Island shute was still being used in August 1942.

An attempt to control the use of unsuitable receptacles for household rubbish came in March 1939, with the attention of householders being drawn to section 5 of the Public Health Act which requires owners and occupiers of buildings to supply suitable covered dustbins, under Corporation Bye Laws which shall be:

[a] constructed of galvanised iron etc.

[b] provided with suitable handles and properly fitted rainproof cover.

At this time there were no problems with sea gulls. They kept very much to the harbour during the day, flying away to the western shores at dusk.

Horses and carts

The main haulage through the town was by horse and cart. There were some lorries but these were not noted for speed.

To get to school, I had to pass Mr. Tucker's pop factory at the top of Fish Street. If you looked inside the door there was always plenty of water splashing about, as men in barwells washed the used bottles, but outside there was often the horse and cart used for delivering. This horse was always stamping the ground, and so many tales were told about him that most children gave the horse a wide berth.

There were a good many fruit and vegetable carts making daily visits with the traders calling out their wares. Some carts were from Penzance and other outlying places, which must have meant an early start. One cart with four twisted brass posts supporting the roof was always worth looking for. Potatoes and apples were sold by the gallon measure.

The fish Jowsters mostly went out of town, or at least Uplong, to sell their fish, not much fish being bought by people Downlong, with the exception of kippers, which were sold from the basket or box of the walking fish hawker.

Almost all traffic Downlong came up over Dick's Hill. Carts with heavy loads used to add a pony, which was tethered to the iron bollard near the Shamrock Lodge. With a vessel discharging coal at the Old Quay most of it came up this way or through Back Road East.

At the start of the herring season flat carts known as net carts brought the nets from the lofts or bark houses to the Quay, or, if the sea was out, to the sand alongside the boats. At the close of the season the nets would be taken to the Island for drying. During a good herring season the farmers would come to town to help land the fish from their pre-arranged boats, and join with the local carts in transporting the fish to the cellars or smokehouses, and the finished article to the railway station.

The delivery from the railway station was by horse and cart, with much jingling of horse brasses. Bread roundsmen and milkmen also had horses, but these were much smaller than the shire horses which pulled sand from Porthmeor beach for the building of the Council houses at Ayr Estate.

West Briton October 1836 *Four Hundred Fish Carts on St. Ives Beach*

So great was the bustle of catching fish and selling mackerel on Sunday that the day had no appearance of the Sabbath, and on Monday as early as two o'clock carts from neighbouring parishes began to arrive and continued throughout the day.

At one time more than 400 carts were on the beach. Messrs. Tremearne, Banfield and Co, commenced the sale of their mackerel, but they raised the price from 24s. per gurry, holding about two hundreds and a half, to 44s. and more than half the carts returned to Redruth, Camborne, Crowan, Gwinear, Phillack, Ludgvan, Marazion, Perran, Towednack, Zennor, St. Just and other parishes, without a supply.

Electricity

The greatest social change came to Downlong with the arrival of electricity in the early nineteen thirties. Before a cable was laid to a house, residents in the street were canvassed to make it a payable proposition for the Power Company to lay their cable. The first to arrive would be a gang of men from the Camborne area to dig up the road. One familiar sight, now something of a rarity, would be the Night Watchman looking after the trench from the privacy of his wooden hut and the heat of his brazier fire. The sight of the Cable Jointer adding a new service to the main cable was always of special interest. Mr. Dick Mann and Mr. Joe Jose became well known with the fishing community, and rarely went home without a "feed of fish" if any were being landed.

To encourage the spreading of the network the Cornwall Electric Power Company were installing three lights and one plug free of charge, the lights being complete with a shade and bulb. The electricity charge for most houses being a quarterly charge of 11s.3d. and a penny per unit. The outbreak of the War stopped many people from having electricity connected, as new connections ceased to be made during the War years, so it took over twenty years for all the houses Downlong to be put on supply.

With electricity and gas becoming available, the days of the slab were numbered. Although an excellent form of heating and cooking in the winter, it could be overpowering in the summer. When blackleaded and the brasswork polished, the slab was a very fine sight, but it entailed a lot of work, together with the extra work any coal fire brings.

27

Slabs were made by local and regional blacksmiths, so could be called Cornish Ranges, but others very similar were used in other parts of the country.

Into the recess vacated by the range, the electric or gas cooker was placed, although in many cases an open tiled grate was fitted, and the cooker put into the smaller back kitchen or scullery. With the loss of the fire, a gas or electric iron had to be purchased. The electric iron had no thermostat control, a tap on the sole plate with the finger being the guide to the heat of the iron.

WE February 1922   Electric Light for all St. Ives?

A meeting to consider the advisability of bringing the electric light into St. Ives was held at Chy-an-Drea Hotel on Wednesday. After a long discussion and the answering of many questions satisfactorily, a Committee was formed to continue negotiations.

WE July 1922   At the July meeting of the Council a letter was read from the Cornwall Electric Power Company [Carn Brea] asking for the consent of the Council to carry mains overhead to St. Ives. Alderman Daniel thought that electricity must come and that they would be foolish to oppose it; "We might agree to overhead mains within a measurable distance of the town, but along the Terrace and in the town they should go underground."

WE October 1926   The Electric Light Company is certainly making a move. Shopkeepers have been approached with a definite offer of a supply by Christmas and apparently Tregenna Hill, High Street and Fore Street are to be supplied with electric current.

St. Ives is one of the very few towns in England where electric light is not available. The 20th century will probably be quoted in history as the electric age, and when current is supplied at a cheap rate, which at present it is not, all classes will benefit greatly by the use thereof.

Electric light will be taking its part in adding to the brightness of our shop windows this Christmastide and will bring its own compensation for the past week's disturbance of Tregenna Hill. Taking everything into considera-

tion, the Electric Company did this very well and it was not for long that the lengthy trench hindered road traffic. One rather envied the man with the cheerful fire on the Hill.

WE November 1926   *Town Council Meeting*
Councillor Freeman said in view of the fact that so many ratepayers of the town were out of work, he thought it was the duty of the Council to do all it could to find work for them. He was given to understand that a job of laying an electric cable in the district started only that morning - several local men asked to be on the job and the Foreman told them he had engaged his own men and they would not be required.

The following letter was proposed to be sent to the Electric Light Co.:- That the St. Ives Town Council who always granted permission for the laying of power cables and give every facility and help, consider that all labour required in connection with the work of the West Cornwall Electric Power Co. in St. Ives and district, should be allocated to the ratepayers of this district. It is not very pleasant to see men from other towns come in to do work, whilst townsmen are standing by out of work.

WE November 1927 *Having installed a powerful electric light in my studio, I am able to take photographs at any time of day or night. The weather makes no difference. Sit early for Christmas.*

Glover, Photographer, Tregenna Hill.

WE Sept 1933   *The cost of electricity.*
In this important matter people living in St. Ives have for some time past been at a decided disadvantage compared with residents at Penzance and other neighbouring towns. The flat rate at St. Ives is 1s.0d. per unit, whereas the price at Penzance has been 10d. To make the comparison worse, this week it was announced that the price at Penzance is to be further reduced to 8d. as from October 1st.

Skeeters and brooms

On Friday evening or Saturday morning the outside of the house had to be cleaned. The windows were "skeeted" with a brass skeeter that would reach the top windows of most houses. This was the favourite job for the boys, and many a householder has been frightened out of his life as water unexpectedly slammed against the window, especially if it was slightly open.

Almost every house had stone steps and a gutter, and these were well broomed down, making sure the water was followed along the road to the nearest drain. This custom is still maintained by a few people Downlong to this present day.

Saturday pennies

Almost every street Downlong had a shop of some kind, mostly they were small grocers who also sold "nicey". Perkins or Small Martins, both in Fore Street, were the most popular. Most nicey were five for a halfpenny. There were also lucky bags and sherbet fountains to attract anyone with a coin to spend.

Most boys had a Saturday job. Some shops had a bike with a basket on the front, but many shops had two-wheeled wooden trucks with two shafts which were easier to push up the hills. Most grocery and shoe shops employed this method of delivery which lasted all the day.

The most usual way to obtain pocket money was to run "arrents" or chop wood for relatives, or, if strong enough, to fetch coal from the coal-yard. This was done by using wooden wheelbarrows which every coal yard possessed and were almost as heavy as the coal. The most reliable source of spending money has always been the Grandparents, and the Saturday penny was forthcoming no matter how slight the gettings.

Saturday evening

Saturday evening was always something special. Instead of playing, as on other weekday evenings, there were certain rituals which had to be followed. First a good wash and change into tidy clothes, the modern jeans would never pass as suitable for going up-town.

For some there was the trip to St. Andrews Street for some "scrowls" from the pork butcher, a pennyworth being enough and to spare, but for most it meant a visit to the chip shop. Fish, chips and peas together with a bottle of pop was a luxury which had been looked forward to all the week, and the cost would be four or five pence.

As a change from chips there would be fritters or tatie cakes as they were also called. These were two a penny. The pop with the glass marble in the top was a penny a bottle and this had come from Mr. Tucker's pop factory at the top of Fish Street.

Chip shops were open all the year round for six evenings a week. The shops up-town were open late on Saturday evenings and the Salvation Army held an open air service in Fore Street beside Simpsons drapery shop. There was therefore plenty of activity. Before shops closed on Saturday evening the blinds or shutters covered the windows and those without these refinements covered their wares with pieces of brown paper or other suitable covers, to show that they were indeed closed on The Lord's Day.

During the winter months the last event of the Saturday evening was the arrival of the Football Herald. In doorways in Tregenna Place and Hill men had been gathering from 10 o'clock to await the paper and to check the football and local rugby results. Although the soccer scores had been broadcast on the radio the rugby scores were not broadcast except for the international games.

At home, jobs had been done with Sunday very much in mind. Shoes were cleaned ready for the morrow, and the pitcher had been filled with water. Whether this was because of the uncertainty of the water supply or because the water would have been lying in lead pipes all night, was never fully explained, but it was a nightly ritual. Everything needed for the Sunday had been bought and even without refrigerators there was no need for shops to open on Sunday.

In the doorway of Mr. Cowling's shop in Fore Street there was a self-service machine with items of grocery in glass fronted compartments. On inserting the correct coin the item could be obtained together with any change required. This was always a source of interest to most children.

Sunday

Sunday was a special day. Apart from a day of worship it was certainly a day of rest. During the herring season men often left their bed on Monday morning and apart from "catching an hour" they had no proper rest until Saturday night, and although there might be no fish in the nets the same work had to be done. Indeed no fish might mean twice the work as the nets were shot again.

Children did not go out to play on Sunday, indeed they never went on the beach, at least not the children I knew.

We had started at Sunday School even before we had attended Day School and we stayed until we were fourteen years of age. Although the families were smaller than in former times, when each School had around 100 children, there were good numbers attending and it was exceptional for a child not to attend.

The Sunday School Anniversary was one of the big Sundays in the year. This was the culmination of all the practices which had been held for many weeks. The piece of poetry or song had to be performed at all three services, everyone being suitably attired in new clothing which had been made or bought specially for the day.

It depended on the religious fervour of the family how many times Chapel was attended during the day. The evening service has always been well attended in most St.

Ives chapels, the gallery always being the popular seats for young men, many having to sink in their seats after a reprimand or a fierce look from the preacher.

I can only speak as far as the hymn books at Zion Chapel were concerned, but it would be safe to say that every blank page inside the front and back covers had either a picture of a mackerel boat under full sail or a piece of poetry which had been pencilled by former generations during dull sermons.

Two pieces have always stuck in my memory, first one of warning : "Black as a raven, black as a rook, black you will be if you steal this book", and the other in lighter vein: "The lightning flashed, the thunder roared and all the earth was shaken. The little pig ran to try to save his bacon". This writing has now ceased. There are no pictures to be found in the books but sadly there are no young men in Zion gallery either.

After Chapel on Sunday evening everyone went "for a round". This was always a walk to Treloyhan, and after passing the Cornish Arms inn one turned down an unnamed lane passing through two kissing-gates together with a few steps to arrive at Hain Walk which was known as "the new road", continuing down over 'Mester hill and into the town. This may well be reversed on the following Sunday, each group greeting other groups as they passed on the way. This custom continued into the blacked- out war years, but has long since ceased. Arriving back on the harbour front during the summer months the Brethren would be holding their own open-air meeting outside Mr. Martin's shop, now Woolworths, and the Salvation Army would be on the lifeboat slip. Those who had not gone for a round would still be walking back and forth on the plat beside the Lodges.

The Lamplighter
The arrival of the Lamplighter at dusk on winter evenings was always of interest to us children. The little flame on

top of the long pole which he used to ignite the gas lamps was always watched in eager anticipation that the wind would blow it out. It never did, so we followed him for a while as he ignited the lamps in the streets around.

The town was entirely lit by gas at this time and most lamps had to be lit and extinguished by the Lamplighter walking around the town. The light we knew best was a much larger lamp on the Primitive Chapel on the Wharf Road. This was lit by its own time switch and lit up the gathering place for many of the winter evening games which started and finished on this spot.

The start of the Second World War saw the removal of the gas lighting, to be replaced at the end of hostilities by electric street lighting, and the disappearance of the ritual of lighting by the Lamplighter with his flickering flame.

In 1939 there were 245 gas lamps in St. Ives and 57 in Carbis Bay. Of these 46 were controlled by clock and 199 were lit by the Lamplighter. At the end of hostilities a few gas lamps were replaced until the Council decided to light the town entirely by electricity. Many of the old gas columns are still in use in the town.

SWS May 1890 The custom of leaving the street lights unlit on moonlit nights and during the summer months is a very long established one. With the Gas works privately owned it was recorded that the light would be discontinued from the 17th May 1890.

WE October 1920 The Council Committee recommended that 30 additional lamps be lit, the lights at the bottom of Fish Street and Bethesda Hill to be lit at once. Councillor Hollow said he hoped there would be a great saving on the lighting account. The Mayor reported that the lamps are never lit on moonlit nights.

WE December 1921 The Gas Manager reported to the Council that 100 street lights were now being lit at the cost of £4.10s. for the season.

WE April 1922 At the Council meeting on 1st April the Councillors heard that street lights were being lit in the town this week but not in the higher parts. Next week it

will be moonlight and none of the lamps will be lit.
WE December 1922 *Although the herring season was nearly over the Council resolved to leave the lamp at Academy Place alight all night for five nights a week during the herring season.*
WE 1928 *No doubt with the visitors in mind public lighting was to commence on the 3rd August.*

Wireless

With the uncertainty of regular money from fishing, and with most homes owning a gramophone, the wireless took a while to get established in the house. There was also some religious doubt about voices coming through the air, as was also felt many years later with the coming of television. Without electricity many found it almost a full time job taking the accumulator to the garage or radio shop for charging every fortnight or so. There was also a small dry battery called a grid bias and a large dry battery which had to be replaced. The aerials were very important for good reception. Insulators separated the aerial from the neighbouring chimney, and brackets held the wire from the facia. Insulated rods took the wire through the window frame, where a lightning switch was fixed to cut off everything should there be lightning around.

As a young boy I can remember at Christmas listening to the Miracle Plays broadcast from St. Hilary Parish church which was under the Pastorate of the Rev. Bernard Walke. He became a national figure for his papal views. These plays were broadcast from 1926 to 1934 and being in local dialect were followed with interest in St. Ives.

The broadcasting of international football on Saturday afternoons brought the first class game into the home. I can remember drawing a plan of the field, divided into eight numbered squares. During the commentary on the game another voice gave the square numbers to help follow the play. The one broadcast which had everyone switching on their sets was after the wreck of the *Alba* in

1938. The Lifeboatmen had gone to London to receive medals and some of them were interviewed on the Saturday night programme *In Town Tonight*. To hear a voice that was known locally was a new experience.

For those without a wireless there was the opportunity to hear international football or special events from a loud-speaker on the porch of the studio occupied by Mr. Carter, now known as "Harbour Amusements" and on the occasion of these broadcasts there was often a large crowd around the porch listening. Although I had heard these broadcasts in the 1930's the following article in the Western Echo under the heading of "Notes about Town" during the 1926 General Strike shows that this had been going on for some years.

"... Many of my readers have expressed their appreciation of the kindness of Mr.J.E.Carter of the Green Studio, The Wharf. This gentleman possesses a very good wireless set and he places the loud speaker on the steps outside his studio so that passers-by may hear the music and the news. During the strike when newspapers were scarce this boon of free wireless news was enjoyed each evening by large crowds of people...".

The application for permission to put aerial wires across roads was almost a regular occurrence at Council meetings but was not always unconditional.

WE March 1926 The Town Clerk reported the receipt of an application from Mr.J.M.Bromley asking permission to fix one end of an aerial wire to the chimney stack at the Harbour Master's Office on Smeaton's Pier and the Committee recommended that the request be agreed subject to the applicant paying a yearly acknowledgment of sixpence and giving a written undertaking to remove the wire immediately the Council required him to do so.

WE 1928 The Finance Committee decided to grant Mr.R.T.Pollard Jnr. permission to put an aerial wire across the road at Back Road West, subject to his giving a written undertaking to remove the wire immediately the Council requires him to do so.

36

The job of selling the wireless brought forth a wealth of information of services available.

WE 1924   *Warren & Ninnes (Central Garage) Ltd., St. Ives*

> *We give you a demonstration*
> *We erect your aerials*
> *We supply your set*
> *We charge your battery*
> *We give all necessary tuition*
> *No previous knowledge of wireless necessary*

WE March 1925   *For those not convinced that they could operate a wireless Mr.S.Blewett gave demonstrations to large audiences in the Public Hall. The instrument used was a two valve Marconiphone and the purity and volume together with absence of Morse interference surpassed expectations.*

WE January 1928   *Mr. M.W.Ninnes of Central Garage made and installed a six-valve set at the Edward Hain Hospital.*

As the wireless rage spread throughout the town, the St. Ives Boys School had an experimental set installed on the 5th December 1928 after raising funds to purchase it through various activities. On the occasion of the Boat Race in March 1929 the Headmaster invited all boys and their parents to come on Saturday at 12.15 to hear the race on the School radio, with the special note that no-one would be admitted before 12 noon or after 12.10.

A strange advert from Mr. J.C.Hollow, Radio Shop, Tregenna Hill in March 1929 is a little difficult to understand and surely must upset those who think we are backward and behind the times in the West:

> **Pictures by wireless.**
> *We can now offer from stock "The Fultograph Outfit"*
> *For receiving pictures on your wireless set.*
> *This is the newest development and pictures are transmitted daily from most of the Power Stations in Europe.*

The equipment was, in fact, an early form of facsimile

machine and unlikely to be found in homes below the Market House.

In 1933 "Here and There" in the Echo published a complaint about wireless oscillation in the Bellair district, only to be followed by more complaints from Tregenna Terrace, and a special request for all to take care not to annoy others with unbearable whistling. In May 1933 St. Ives broke new ground when the St. Ives Chamber of Commerce advertised the town on Radio Fecamp on a Sunday evening. Included in the advert was a reference to the ultra violet rays which were recorded in a league table in the national newspapers and of which St. Ives was often near the top. Out of 36 towns in Great Britain measuring radiation in 1930 St. Ives headed the list for five months in succession.

> *"St. Ives in Cornwall leads the way*
> *For the health giving ultra violet ray*
> *For a real beneficial holiday*
> *Go to St. Ives Cornwall"*

Conveniences

In a town where stone was the main building material it is strange that the public conveniences were built with brick. There was one between the Rose Lodge and the Shore Shelter Lodge, another at the eastern entrance to Porthmeor beach, and at the bottom of the Meadow overlooking Porthmeor beach. These have all been removed and replaced by others tucked away in more secluded places, and are now for ladies as well as gentlemen.

There were no bolts or coin slots, and no paper was provided except newspaper which had been brought to the place by previous users. There was a square hole cut in each cubicle door and this would be covered by a coat or other item of clothing to show that it was occupied. A long leg was also required to keep the door closed.

There was no vandalism, in fact we hadn't heard of the word. There was also no shortage of customers as there were many more men at work in the harbour area and not every house had a lavatory.

Until the end of the second world war the majority of the paper used in all toilets was newspaper. It was a regular task to fold and cut newspaper into squares, and after piercing one corner with a skewer, a piece of string was threaded through for hanging. The only time we had coloured paper was when we used an old Football Herald, which used to be pink.

WE March 1930 New public conveniences are to be erected at the West Pier and these will include modern ladies' and gents' lavatories etc. Other conveniences are to be constructed at the Island and Clodgy. These will be fitted with automatic slot locks and therefore are likely to be revenue producing.

WE December 1937 At the Council meeting Councillors Sullivan and Long protested against the removal of a convenience next to the Rose Lodge, but it was explained by Councillor Best that the old structure was a disgrace. The fishermen were in agreement that it should be removed.

"Specs" for all

In the age of fluorescent light it is difficult to imagine how people could read, sew and knit in a small light given by a candle or an oil lamp, but as in all ages, eye-sight often deteriorates. Today this means expensive glasses involving more expense after a few years as eyesight further deteriorates. As a boy I remember going to Penzance, and in Woolworth's there were always a number of people trying on spectacles, looking at a printed card. A suitable pair was selected and the delighted customer paid only a small amount. At that time Woolworth's was known as the Threepenny and Sixpenny stores, so the "specs" would have been quite cheap and certainly satisfied a need that would never have been met from any other source.

Swindoners

Among the first to come to St. Ives were the Great Western Railway people from Swindon. Taking advantage of their concessionary travel they were almost the first to discover St. Ives and it also gave them a long ride on the G.W.R. network. Local people who had "Swindoners" coming went to the railway station to meet them. They arrived about six or seven o'clock in the morning and were helped through the town with their cases, coming to the same houses year after year. Many who came to St. Ives as children were still coming with their own children when Swindon week had stretched to Swindon fortnight. In most cases it was the houses Downlong who took these working people in, but all the clubs such as cricket, tennis and swimming put on events for their entertainment.

At this time in the holiday trade it was "rooms and attendance", the housewives cooking any foodstuffs the guests brought in, therefore it was only to be expected that mackerel, which were almost given away, would be high on the list, and usually someone with all his fingers loaded with mackerel would arrive at the door during the evening requesting mackerel for supper. Although these visitors were not lodgers as such it was usual for boys to ask each other if they had any lodgers in.

The big event of the week was the Saturday when almost everyone went to the Malakoff to see the train with two engines and twelve coaches take them back to Swindon. It also brought the fine weather again as it often rained during Swindon week.

WE On July 9th 1921 300 to 400 visitors arrived from Swindon.

In 1923 the number had risen to 800 by special train.

WE 1924 On what was described as the world's biggest excursion 29,000 people left Swindon on 31 trains (520 coaches) on the Great Western Railway system - of these 955 came to St. Ives.

Pop and ice cream

A new sight to be seen each Saturday was a *Corona* lorry from Camborne delivering wooden cases of four large bottles of pop from house to house as required. Previous to this we had only seen Mr. Tucker's pop, which had a glass marble in the top of each bottle. Now we had clip-on tops and the four bottles with a case to keep them in cost one shilling and ninepence including the deposit on the case.

A new scene now appeared on the harbour front when tricycles bearing the name T.Wall appeared, selling ice cream. For a halfpenny there was a three sided cardboard tube filled with coloured ice. A rumour went around, which must have slowed their business, that these were made with sweepings of ice from the factory floor, but they tasted alright.

Most children bought their ices from one of Mr. Hart's carts. A halfpenny cornet was the usual buy, and if funds were flush a penny cornet or wafer, while if fishing was good the men landing the fish would sometimes be seen to have a 'tuppeny sandwich', which entailed opening the mouth rather wide in order to bite.

WE January 1910   PURE DRINKS.

We are the makers of the purest mineral waters offered to the public. Every bottle we supply is made from the purest water and no injurious chemicals whatever are used.

All our beverages are manufactured with the purest and best ingredients that can possibly be obtained, and by up-to-date machinery. No water used until thoroughly filtered.

J.Tucker and Son, Back Road, St. Ives.

N.B. J.T.& S. beg to draw the attention of their customers to the necessity of returning all empty bottles promptly. Any persons wilfully smashing or wrongfully using any mineral water bottles are liable to be prosecuted.

WE May 1935   BOROUGH OF ST. IVES

Tenders are invited from Ice Cream Vendors for the fol-

41

lowing sites as pitches for Ice Cream stands.

Westcott's Quay	*2 barrows*
Bathing steps, Porthminster	*2 barrows*
Malakoff recess	*1 barrow*
Top of Skidden Hill	*1 barrow*
Man's Head	*1 barrow*
Ventnor Well	*1 barrow*
Island Gate	*1 barrow*
Smeaton's Pier	*1 barrow*
North of lifeboat slip	*1 barrow*
Corner of No.1 fish plot	*1 barrow*
West Pier	*1 barrow*

The gas works

The gas works played its part in the life of the town. Apart from the supply of gas, bags of coke could be bought there to be used in open fires in sitting rooms or bedrooms. Tar was also sold for use on walls, or especially on boats. To help our education we went from school to look over the whole works to see how gas was produced. It was always a big user of coal which came by ship to Smeaton's Pier or to the railway station. This was used in its furnaces.

Apart from everything else, the main attraction at the gas works was a man called Cap'n Paynter, known as Man Friday to the general public. He slept in the works and no doubt the dust helped him to earn his nickname. His stories were told in all seriousness to any who would listen. He had sailed in ships with cargoes of small green men, umbrella seed etc. He had sailed on the same tack so long that the ship's side had worn through. His most famous story was when the mate with a full set of whiskers went on to the foredeck and the wind blew his whiskers off, only to stick to the chin of Cap'n Paynter who happened to be on the bridge. His face still survives in pictures and a well-known Kodak advertisement, but alas most of his stories have been lost. Thomas Bassett Paynter died in March 1941 aged 76 years.

The St. Ives gas works was built almost on the edge of the town. The foundation stone was laid on the 19th May 1835. It was built by masons from Camborne as the St. Ives men were asking one third more to do the job. They must have done a quick job as the town was lit by gas on the 1st December of that year. One of the first places to benefit was the lighthouse on Smeaton's Pier, which had previously been lit by candles. Soon the street lights were fitted, but they were extinguished during moonlit nights and during the summer months, from the 17th May 1890. The private Company running the gas works was taken over in 1895 by the Town Council on a Provisional Order known as the St. Ives (Cornwall) Gas Order of 1895. In the year ending 31st March 1901 gas made amounted to 7,300,000 cubic feet compared with 1935 when it was 37,600,000 cubic feet.

WE May 1924 The Gas Committee of the Council recommended a wage rise to one of the fitters, from one shilling and a penny- halfpenny to one shilling and threepence per hour. The Gas Manager's salary to be increased to £275 per annum.

WE November 1925 The Gas Committee recommended in consideration of 12 applications for gas to be supplied to their houses, that the gas main be laid in Victoria Hill as soon as convenient. The outlay of £40, with 12 new consumers, promised to be a paying proposition.

The 7th January 1933 saw the completion of an up-to-date plant. It had taken eight months to build, giving work to a number of local men. The official opening was on Wednesday 11th October by the Rt. Hon.Walter Runciman LLD, MP for St. Ives and President of the Board of Trade. It was a self-contained, 80 feet high structure with three retorts, steel framed, brick lined with a high chimney which stood out above the skyline. Two conventional gas holders were overshadowed by a cylindrical holder which looked like a giant airship. The bomb which landed on the gasholder during the war made a mess of the works, but all was put back into working order. It has now been totally removed, the giant zeppelin disappearing under the cutter's torch in April 1985.

Gone dead

There must be very few towns in the world in which the news of a bereavement spreads so quickly. The use of the card nailed to the fishermens' Lodge and placed in shop windows, announcing the time and place of the funeral, has few equals. For those connected with or respected by the fishing community, the flags are flown at half-mast on the Lodges.

Two things in recent years have upset the traditional St. Ives funeral. Firstly the ceasing of Saturday and Sunday burials, and the opening of Longstone Cemetery at Carbis Bay. It was an accepted thing that if possible all funerals would be on Sunday, when more people could show their respect. Also, walking funerals depended on plenty of manpower to carry the coffin to the Chapel and then on to Barnoon Cemetery.

With new regulations robbing many St. Ives people of their last resting place, together with the need for cars to be able to attend, the number of people who would normally go to the graveside has dropped to almost family only, whereas in former times there would be scores, especially for anyone connected with the fishery.

The show of mourning lasted much longer as well. Black was worn by the family attending the funeral, as well as by the widow for the next twelve months. For those with light coats a black diamond was worn on the top sleeve. Flags were flown at half mast on any boats owned by the family. Also, immediate family curtailed their social activities while the deceased was lying dead.

The expression "gone dead" was often used by older persons. It was a time of great friendship by neighbours and friends.

WE 1919 The Cemetery Committee of the Council decided to ask the Home Secretary to sanction the following fees being paid to Ministers conducting funerals :-
Morning service   4s.6d.
Afternoon service 2s.6d.
WE 1930 At a Council meeting Councillor Bryant wanted to know if it was possible to make a bye-law prohibiting the carrying of an empty coffin through the streets unless it was covered. He did not think the present practice was decent or becoming.

Alderman Warren said they prided themselves on keeping the Sunday. Efforts should be made for all Sunday funerals to be in the mornings. As it was, the man at the cemetery was employed all day, but mention was made of the extra fee for morning burials.

It had always been traditional for a group of men to precede the coffin at funerals. At a given signal there would be a change of bearers, until finally the graveside was reached. Suitable hymns were often sung during the journey. The hard labour for the bearers was eased by horse drawn hearses for those who could afford them, but the following advertisement in the Western Echo in 1935 shows that change reaches all professions:
To undertakers and others.
For hire, modern saloon type motor hearse.
Warrens Tours, West Pier Garage.

WE MILLBAY CLEANING & DYE WORKS
Hourly black dyeing.
Every hour we start a fresh vat and keep a staff of finishers, who do nothing else but mourning orders, so that for 12s.0d. we can return your costume or suit to you dyed a clear crisp black, and finished so well that an expert would be puzzled to tell the difference between it and new.
SWS May 1900 THINGS SEEN AND HEARD, by Observer.
That the mortuary chapels at St. Ives cemetery were built between 40 and 50 years ago, and during that time, it

is said, the doors, windows etc have not had a coat of paint.

SWS November 1900 *The funeral of Mr. Henry Trevorrow of Court Cocking, took place on Sunday afternoon. A large number of relatives and friends attended the last sad rite. The Primitive Methodist Choir and Sunday School were in attendance and sang suitable hymns en route to the cemetery.*

In spite of the rhyme, each wife did not have seven cats, but this picture
shows that in the 1930's each house had one cat. A cat was necessary to
prevent mice causing damage to fishing nets stored in the cellar.

Crew of the St. Ives fishing boat *Sheerness* 1930.
William John Stevens, Edward Murt,
Matthew Stevens Jnr., Henry Perkin, Joel Perkin, Francis Stevens.

Dressed in the fashion of the day, Aunt Mary (left) and my Mother have taken me to Porthminster Hill to await the train coming under the bridge and envelop us in smoke and steam. *1929.*

A heavy washday at Bethesda Place is drying free from all traffic.

A freshly oiled oilskin frock and a pair of leather seaboots shining under a fresh application of tallow, indicate the occupation of the householder.

Two pairs of freshly tallowed leather sea-boots stand amongst assorted washing in St. Eia Street. Below the stone steps were lofts and cellars, some containing concrete tanks which were filled with pilchards being pressed for export.

Porthmeor Square with its gas lantern, *c1930*. One of the few houses Downlong to boast a front garden. The scraper on the third step shows a sense of humour by the owner, but was no doubt to remove leather sea-boots.

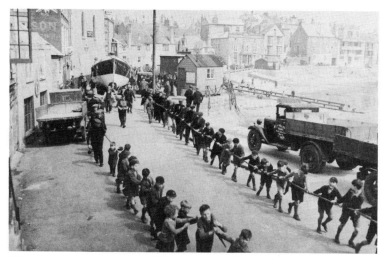

Whether in the way, or of some help, boys were always encouraged to pull on the lifeboat hawsers. The armbands, known as badges, were thrown from the window over the lifeboat house on the occasion of a launch, and payment was made on their return to the boathouse. Here the *Caroline Parsons* is being put back on station. *c1936*.

The broken remains of the *Caroline Parsons* on the Island rocks with the *Alba* acting as a breakwater on the morning after her stranding on the night of 31st January 1938. Without the bravery of the men on the shoreline there would have been many more drowned on that occasion.

Dick's Hill, or Fish Street if you prefer. A cobbled street in this picture, *c1900*, which has undergone great changes, especially in the 1920's and 30's. From where the mats are drying on the wall to the harbour all has been removed at different times.

St. Lukes Court makes a quiet spot to dry the washing. The shared tap at the top of the steps was the only water supply. The houses at the back were removed to make part of the Wharf car park when the houses in Water Lane, Norway and Pudding Bag Lane were cleared. *c.1935.*

Form 6, Mr. Lawry's class of 1939 at the Stennack School. Back row: J. Berriman, E. Bennetts, The Author, K. Penberthy, E. Fuller, G. Bailey, J. Richards, D. Parker. Second row: Mr. Lawry, J. Curnow, J. Burt, J. Stephenson, R. Kemp, H. Williams, P. Cortis, J. Stevens, G. Thomas, D. Curnow, J. B. Stevens. Third row: F. Uren, C. Bennetts, D. Perkin, T. Stratton, T. H. Lander, L. Date, D. Hodge, W. Pope, E. Thomas, H. Peters. Front: J. D. Stevens, A. Hollow, P. H. Rouncefield, C. Dunn, J. V. Trevorrow, G. Wearne, M. Taylor.

The chimney at Cryséde (pronounced Chris-aid) silk printing factory belches smoke and their surplus dye colours the sea at Porthmeor beach. Washing is laid out to dry on the Island and visiting campers have the western side for their bell tents. c1937.

Capt. Paynter (Man Friday), the teller of tales who slept in the Gas Works. The man leaning against the wall is Frankie Ivory who told fortunes. The brick building is the men's public toilet – there were no such conveniences for ladies. *c1935*.

Rays were dried against the wall, not only for home consumption, but as a business venture to be hawked around the town.

Tom Northcote's quay with a pole at the end. The quay has in recent years received some attention but was threatened at one time as the site of a car park on steel piles. Tom was a local fisherman but why his name is associated with the quay is uncertain. *c1930.*

From left to right: James, Richard, Edward and Mike Peters, hauling crab nets on the gig *Coronia,* display their barwells and an oilskin frock probably made by their wives from unbleached calico cloth. White rubber seaboots have replaced the locally made leather ones. *1933.*

The Gas Works which was built on the western outskirts of the town overshadows the houses in The Meadow. This building and the retaining wall by 'Sunset', were among the things blamed for the build-up of sand which threatened to overwhelm many properties at different times. *c1937.*

Mountains of sand which blew over the rooftops as far as the bottom of Bunkers Hill and Digey–Fore Street corner, and had to be periodically removed and flattened by bulldozers. *1950.*

3 GROWING UP

The Board School (Infants)

The time eventually came for the move from the Island Road School to the Board School at the Stennack. This school was divided into the Big Boys, the Infants and the Big Girls. To go so far up the Stennack was quite an adventure for most of us. Except for Good Friday when we went to Consol's pool to sail our boats this was new ground for most.

The Headmistress was Miss Dufty who had been there for many years. With the change of school came the change to pencil and paper and later to pen and ink and the wonder of 'double writing'. It is difficult to remember any special thing that happened except for Friday afternoon. This was for indoor games and Maypole dancing, everyone being rewarded with a sticky raspberry flavoured sweet from a large tin. These were known as 'fun sweets'.

Occasionally while in the playground we saw the rear view of Mr. Bray, the Headmaster of the Big Boys, complete with cap and gown. We were warned by older boys of the fate that awaited us when our turn came to move next door. This occasion was never to arise for in November 1933 Mr. Bastian moved from Trevarrack School to the Headship of the Boys School in the Stennack.

The railway

The children of the town stayed very much in their own area to play but as babies in prams they would certainly have been taken to the railway station to see the train.

There was always something of interest for parent and child. The first view was the train stopping at the bridge before its slow approach into the station, the Signalman taking up a position near the track to receive the metal

47

token from the Fireman. This represented the Driver's authority to be on the single line from St. Erth.

The uncoupling of the engine midst a cloud of steam was followed by toots from the engine as it steamed towards the town then reversed on a second track to be coupled up to the other end of the train for the return journey to St. Erth. Mr. Charlie Mitchell was one of the Drivers and he was a great favourite, often lifting children into the cab to see all the sights there.

Everything seemed so permanent at the station that it was a great shock to see almost everything disappear. The granite station building with its waiting room, ticket office, toilets and bookstall, the crane and goods sidings, the water tower, the engine shed and the track which ran almost to the steps down into the Warren. No longer will children run up 'Mester hill to stand on the road bridge to be enveloped in smoke and steam as the train passes underneath.

Trains still come and go, but with the absence of steam there must be very little to attract parent or child to the railway station as in former days.

The railway at St. Ives was officially opened on the 24th May 1877, being the last railway built to Brunel's broad gauge of seven feet and a quarter of an inch. This was changed to the standard gauge of four feet eight and a half inches in the gauge conversion of May 1892.

SWS June 1889 *A letter complains of the brutal carelessness of the railway contractor in allowing hundreds of tons of debris to be shot down the hill slope at each end of the little bay.*

SWS In the herring season of 1899 four or five fish trains of 100 to 340 tons were being despatched daily. During a particularly heavy two days 550 tons were sent away, with the fish bringing the general price of 1s.0d. for 120. It is obvious that the railway people were the only ones making money from the heaviest landings St. Ives has ever known.

Children playing

The weather was not always suitable for children to play on the Island or the beaches. Young children played very much in their own part of the town. Only as they became bigger did they venture into other parts of Downlong and were well grown before going Uplong for any reason at all.

If there was an illness of a severe nature a cart load of sand was spread outside the house of the sick. This was to deaden the sound of the horse and carts and was an area to play well away from.

During the herring season of November and December many men would go to bed in the afternoon to catch an hour. Playing children would soon be warned off with the cry: "There are men turned in" or the other favourite which has outlived the herring: "Go and play in front of your own front door". Fortunately it was only necessary to play on the streets during the winter months. We had the finest of adventure playgrounds within minutes walk of most.

SWS November 1908   At the meeting of the St. Ives Town Council on Monday evening, Councillor J.Ninnis said there had been great complaints recently of hawkers shouting at the top of their voices thus causing great annoyance to fishermen who wanted to sleep. The fishermen at this season of the year were obliged to take their rest in the day time. The matter was referred to the Watch Committee and Councillor G.Williams remarked that he wished the Committee would also take into consideration the speed of motor cars travelling through the narrow streets of the town.

Games and pastimes

The one word used since the last war to account for vandalism by young people has been boredom. "Nothing for the youngsters to do" has been the excuse to open all kinds of clubs for a generation that has lost its ability to make its

49

own fun without a lot of money being spent or damage being done. Taking any period up to the end of the war, street games were very cheap and had their own seasons, but I can only write of the games played Downlong.

The piece of road between the Rose Lodge and the Primitive Chapel was a starting place for most of the games of "sides". This was because of the very big gas light fixed on the Chapel wall, which made it a good starting place and "home" for the winter game played by two sides with up to a dozen players a side. After deciding which side would hide, those who were hiding found their way to the darkest places of the town. The Ropewalk and Piazza studios were favourite places, but any loft door or pile of gurries or fish boxes was also suitable. After counting up to 100 the other side would come searching. After hiding in a stinking gurry or being frightened to death whilst hiding in some dark loft where every sound made one's hair stand on end, it was often a relief to be caught. When some had been caught and a few had sneaked "home" the cry of: "All in, all in" would echo across the harbour and heads would pop up from all sorts of hiding places, even from barrels stacked up against the Chapel wall. The sides then reversed, with the hunters being hunted, and so another evening was spent with good fun but no damage or expense.

One game which had a very long history in the town was marbles. Having been played by men in former times it was a boys' game in the period about which I am writing, and it often co-incided with rain. It was played in the gutters on the way to school, in the playground, and in the gutter all the way home again. This game also had a language of its own with words like try taw, stonehead, footching, chalkerds, heights and other words known only to the players of earlier generations and handed down without any explanation of their origins.

There was one game which started in a ring containing marbles which were fired at by glass alleys and which continued by firing at the opponent's marbles along the gutter. Although it was only made of plain glass one way of getting a marble was to break a pop bottle or a visit to the pop factory in Fish Street where a few marbles could be obtained.

If it rained too hard for marbles there was always boat racing. The gutter in Bedford Road was excellent for this game. With a matchstick each for a boat many a boy has been late home for dinner after watching his boat shooting the rapids in the race to the drain at the bottom of Bedford Road. This game would be classed as unhygienic now. Perhaps this is why many of the fine granite gutters of the town have been covered with tarred gravel, but we enjoyed the fun, and the harder it rained the faster the boats travelled.

The season for games did not last long enough to bore anyone. Hoops were played by girls and boys, wooden hoops propelled by hand or by a piece of stick were for the girls, while for the boys iron hoops were made by the Blacksmith complete with a drill to trickle it, for a few pence. Boys would go as far as Treloyhan and trickle hoops all the way to the harbour. In the season when the hoops were in full swing the Wharf could be as dangerous as in the skate board age.

Tops was also a game for boys and girls. The girls tops were started with a whip and hopefully kept going by whipping. Peg tops were wrapped around with string and thrown. It always seemed to be the aim for some boys to split other tops by striking them with the spills of their own tops when thrown.

The most enjoyable and possibly most dangerous pastime was riding a trolley. It was made from a box, a plank of wood, four wheels on two pram axles and some nails. The driver sat in the box with his feet on the front axle. He also had a rope on the axle to steer with. The passenger on the back pushed when on level ground, then jumped on board when going downhill. Some models had a brake on the back wheel, also a jam jar and candle on the running board for night driving. The ride from the Island Church down to the gun, then down to the Island gate, was a favourite, but was rarely undertaken without a spill.

Although boys rarely ventured out of town the exception was to go to St. Erth marshes to pick bullrushes to dry and soak in paraffin for Guy Fawkes night.

A near relative to the trolley was the two wheel truck. These could be used either for fun or for the cartage of goods. With a rope rein around the shoulder of the "horse" held by the passenger, good fun could be obtained until it was time to change places.

Just before the war two-wheel scooters were very popular. For 12s.6d. (62 and a half pence) a spoked wheel model with brake, or a solid wheel at 10 shillings (50p) could be bought, but this amount of money was not very plentiful. Bigger boys would often request rides and it sometimes took quite a while to get the scooter back. There was also the story that this type of exercise made one leg longer than the other, but perhaps with so many cobbles no one has noticed.

A boys' game with two teams of five or more was "Pomperino". One boy stood against the wall and was known as the pillow. The rest of the team would then bend down head to tail in a line and the other team would then jump as far as possible along the backs. If the bottom team collapsed there would be cries of "Wake hoss" (weak horse) and the jumping team would then jump again. If the feet of the jumping team touched ground they would then have to change positions. This game was played in the school playground, but very often on the foreshore sand encouraged by the onlookers and accompanied by shouts of "Pomperino" as each jumper landed with a thud which shook the sand as well as the contestants.

The game of "Duck" had been played on the harbour sand for many years, often watched by interested spectators outside the Lodges. Seven or eight tin cans were arranged to stand on top of one another and were known as the Duck. One boy would stand as close as he dared and the others would then throw stones until the Duck was knocked down. While the Duck was rebuilt the others retrieved their stones. If on the completion of the rebuilding a thrower was touched before he collected all his stones he then changed places and stood near the Duck. Different generations had variations of the rules, but the expression: "The Duck is down" still covers the collapse of any items or objects in the minds of older people of this town.

For those with a sharp knife and a suitable piece of wood, there was always the fun of making a "Whizabout", a two bladed propellor, often with coloured rings and a nail through the middle. This was fixed to a stick or the front of a bike or scooter.

On a windy day home-made parachutes were thrown from the Church on the Island or from the rocks at Carncrows, to float down to the dump and pig scrows below.

When one adds all these games and pastimes to the others common to any fishing port it will be seen that there was not much time left in which to get bored.

SWS October 1901 *The two great Autumn games, football and marbles, have commenced at St. Ives. Old men, young men and children join in the latter game and the weather makes no difference, the dirtier the roads the better.*

Sand and sea

'Meor and 'Widden beaches were the places where most of the school holiday was spent. Tents were built with hessian, matting and canvas. These were surrounded by a wall of sand, reinforced by bed iron from Breakwater. Everyone played in their own area, and the only time we went to other areas was to bombard other camps with tubbans of grass or ore weed cut into three inch lengths. This would be a retaliatory raid for one that we had received, probably from "The Arches" gang, who were our most regular opponents. No-one ever raised any objection to the tents and except for when we had to strip the site for a high tide the camp was there for the summer.

On 'Meor the bathing huts were on wheels and were pulled down to the tide mark each day, and then up to the wall at the close of day. Mothers used to bring their knitting and sit in groups against the wall all the afternoon, only visiting people being in the area from the middle of the beach across to the western end. The tents and bathing machines were owned by two different proprietors, Mr. Care having the middle and Mr. James looking after the western end. Although there were few people in the water it must be assumed that the rip tides were there, but we had no lifeguards to point them out, and except for a little girl who was drowned on August Bank Holiday years before, after getting entangled with the weed around Gowna rock, the only other drownings were during the war years when the Commandos trained there. Perhaps it would be only right to say that without the lethal Malibu boards, we were able to bathe well away from the rocks, and many of the young men at that time were strong swimmers.

'Widden beach had its own regulars who visited each day, erected their tents, and enjoyed their birthright among much rubbish that was continually thrown onto the sand and rocks. To those who went there these were happy days. It is strange that in recent years since the site has been cleaned and developed very few local people ever use the beach.

Children were never idle on the sand. Apart from bathing, the main activity was for the girls to play shops and boys to "tack" boats. First of all a tin had to be found that would rip down the join and separate from the bottom. A stone was required to help fold the piece of tin the length of the boat. The bow and stern were then folded over and all folds given a good banging to make waterproof. The tin then opened into the shape of a boat. After filling with damp sand all the other parts of the boat were added according to taste. A matchbox for a wheelhouse, pieces of wood for masts and mizzen boom, seaweed bladders for buoys, and a piece of bark rubbed into shape for a punt added to the fun. The removal of a handful of sand made a net room which was filled with old net. To add to the novelty this net was often caught on fire. Although not sure of the reason for this it certainly left its mark and there is no smell quite like it. With the completion of the boats it took only a few minutes to complete a harbour with two piers and a slipway. The boats would then be tacked over the waves of dry sand by pushing the stern between the thumb and first finger. This probably lasted all day with boats breaking down and being towed back, shipwrecks and battles, according to the type of boat being made. After tiring of tacking, the boat would be emptied and a mast complete with cardboard sail would be forced into the bow fold, a stone would be placed in the stern, and after a trial in a pool, the boat would then be sent to sea. After a while someone would aim a stone. This would soon be followed by a bombardment, and "finis" for the boat as it disappeared under the water, a new day bringing a new boat according to the size of the tin. It is strange that during the war years when the beaches were not used, the knack of making these boats was lost to local boys, although there are more tins about now than we ever had.

Another type of boat which has been made for generations is the Corken Barber from the Cornish Cokyn Baba, a small boat. These were for sailing in the harbour or across 'Widden from the Island to the Breakwater. The materials required were a piece of cork, a piece of hoop iron from a barrel and a piece of plywood from a tea chest, alas all now in short supply, but very plentiful in former times.

Finding a cork on the tide-mark or in the loft, was the start. Shaping into the shape of a boat only took a few minutes, cutting three crosses in the deck for the sails and a slot for the jib took only a few more minutes. This was followed by a slot for the keel of hoop iron or slate. In former days sails were made from chips of wood, with top sails fitted to them, but with plywood being more plentiful and lighter, we always used a layer of ply. After assembling, the boat was thrown into a pool to test its stability. After any necessary adjustments she would then "sail like a whiff" across the harbour, often followed by a punt. A variation of this boat would be the flat cork with two sails set in a butterfly rig. These would only sail with the wind, whilst the former could sail into it.

Those with very sharp knives would make a boat from a piece of broom handle. After shaping and slotting, five or six sails were fitted according to the length. This was called a chip and sailer by us boys, but the origin of the name was not known to us.

The total tools required for making all three boats were a knife and a stone, the materials all coming from the tidemark or the breakwater rubbish tips.

With the maximum fine of £400 for allowing a dog to go on to Porthmeor Beach from 1985, it would be hard to imagine what fate would befall half a dozen boys tacking boats, pouring out smoke from burning net. No doubt they would be banned, after being picked up by the "tin boat warden"'.

From the middle of the beach to the Island, the Council or its beach lessees have never shown much interest. For some unknown reason during the war years the sand built up against the houses and studios, and in time rooms were under the sand which had reached roof level. This spilled over into Back Road West and into the Digey and became a problem. People were having difficulty in getting past the Meadow without being temporarily blinded by sand. Householders fought a lone but futile battle to keep the sand from burying their property while the town wanted these people to give up their rights, if any, to a strip of beach adjoining their property. After a lot of negotiations and arguments that the sand was coming from the Council's part of the beach, and when the town was in danger of being cut in two by the sand being blown as far as the harbour, a bulldozer was hired to alleviate the danger. This means has had to be employed several times since, before it reached danger proportions.

WE 8 July 1911   *Visitors can now be provided with*
   Bathing tents, bathing machines,
   Bathing costumes, deck chairs, on Porthmeor Beach
   Bathing costumes and towels from 1 penny each
   Bathing machines 3 pence each. Children 2 pence.
   Deck chairs 1 penny.

Porthmeor is one of the finest bathing beaches in Cornwall, and being open to the broad Atlantic the water is fresh and buoyant, and free from any objectionable taste.

   Ask for John Care (late Tent Proprietor at Porthminster) Virgin Street, St. Ives.

The Island

The Island has always been a favourite playground for children of every generation, but age was no barrier to playing games of football and cricket on the "Meadow" now taken as a car park, or the western side of the Island, now faced with expensive windows of luxury flats.

One of the finest playthings on the Island was a German field gun placed on the top near the house. This gun was always "in action" until it was removed for scrap during the second world war - one wonders if it finished its travelling as a bomb in its country of origin.

"Blood and flesh" cave was always a draw to boys. The story of a passage leading to the Church on top has been handed down through the years. Armed with a candle and matches many expeditions have sought this passage, which would be worth a fortune to the modern town, but all attempts have failed.

The headless horseman on a white horse, who roams the Island on certain nights, has always been a deterrent to going on the headland at night. Many stories of this phantom exist, but possibly he has disappeared with the coming of the motor car.

The western slope and rocks were the drying ground for pickled ropes and nets. This was one part to keep away from. The pickle burnt the skin and was difficult to remove from clothing. At the close of a drift net fishing season the Island was covered with nets being dried before being taken to the lofts for mending and storing. The cork ropes were often kept off the grass with baskets. There was a great temptation for boys to crawl under the nets, and if nets barred the passage when playing, a walk across the top soon brought a shout from some hitherto unseen fisherman to get off and on to the little remaining grass, which often meant a long detour.

With nets on the Island there would be net carts in the Meadow. These were used as slides, but the more venture-some would remove an iron pin and a slide became a see-saw. This did no good to the cart and shook every bone in the body.

The front slope was always the drying ground for washing. The washing was kept in place with stones on the corners, and this was a place to be avoided. The flasket was often left with the clothes, and anyone getting close to either soon got a warning shout from the direction of Island Road.

Tents were very popular during the summer season. Local boys made tents from hessian and sailcloth. These were for day use only.

The pole used by the Coastguards to practise their life-saving was situated just above the ruins of the old cow house overlooking 'Widden beach. A rope attached to the top gave a ride in decreasing circles for those with a head for that kind of travel.

A piece of cardboard or lino could mean hours of fun sliding down the slopes at the front or the back until pants were worn thin or the sun had set.

Gardens were unknown to most children Downlong, so little patches of earth under the ridge of boulders found on the Island were made into gardens by children transplanting daisy or celandine plants to those sheltered positions.

The arrival of warm evenings was often the signal for the arrival of the flying beetles known to us as 'dumble dories'. These are rarely found in other parts of the town. Their arrival was usually heralded by screams of the girls trying to remove them from their hair. When put into a matchbox they were supposed to disappear by the morning, but few would handle the insects to test the truth of the story.

According to John Leland in 1538 there was a Chapel of St. Nicholas and a pharos for light at the point of Pendinas, the old name for the Island. There was also a warning beacon of furze to be lit on sighting enemy ships, the Borough accounts for 1665-6 show the expenditure of 1s.9d. for ropes, straw and furze. The rock near the Coastguard lookout is shown on old maps as "Lamp Rock".

In September 1860 the new fort at St. Ives fired its first shots. Whilst it was intended to fire at two barrels this was changed to a rock at 1500 yards. A 68 pound ball passed close over the rock from the large gun. The small guns were then fired. One of the shells bounced off the sea and exploded on the mainland near some cows.

When estimates were being made to provide a lighthouse to mark the Stones reef, the Board of Trade enquired from the War Department in November 1856 if the lighthouse, now known as Godrevy, could be built on the Island which would entail moving the existing Fort. The War Office refused this and offered two other sites which were declined by their Lordships in case of damage when the guns were fired.

WE March 1919 The Admiralty huts recently erected on the Island have been acquired by the Cornwall Sanatorium Committee for erection at Tehidy.

WE February 1920 The German gun allocated to St. Ives as a war trophy arrived last week and has been placed on the Island.

WE April 1940 The Highways and Town Improvement Committee of the St. Ives Town Council discussed camping on the Island during the coming season. The rate for visiting tents to be 1s.3d. per night. For local tents 1s.0d. per tent weekly.

Playing places

It is no good to have games to play unless there is somewhere to play them. The Island has already been mentioned; the sand was accepted for many games, but a place which was always popular for cricket, football, duck, marbles, hoops, scooters, as well as being a good hiding place, was a road known as the Ropewalk. This is a very rough road from the Island Road School to Porthmeor Road. The road was the site of a former ropewalk but had never been used as such in this century. One good thing about it was the absence of any glass in the windows. During the herring season there was the smell of oak- flavoured smoke from kipper houses on both sides, but the road surface has never changed.

During the herring season the Wharf Road was full of barrels, boxes and gurries. These were used for hiding places, and also re-arranged so that it was possible to crawl into the pile and come out on the other side. This was good fun, but it left its mark on clothing, stinking with fish and covered with "shales".

One of the best places to play was in the "Chaaple" or, to use its correct name, St. Leonard's Chapel at the top of Smeaton's Pier. This had been used for boxing for many years. It still has a "knuckle hole" showing that marbles had been played there many years ago, but there was always a rope swing hanging from beam to beam. Climbing from beam to beam was very popular. During rainy weather it was often full of children. Fishermen also used it as a meeting place and shelter. It was very dark there and, to be fair, had a very strong smell at the darkest end. It may have been a chapel at some time, but to us it was somewhere to play, and as far as I can remember, it had no door, so access was possible at all times.

While many games started from the Wharf there were also other places where children met. Island Square was often home for the game of sides. Some of the hiding places around the lofts and studios were very dark. Of course there were hundreds of cats as well, and any sound was enough to make one's hair stand on end.

Knocking doors and breaking jam jars near a window had been handed down, also tying two doors together and knocking both at the same time. This sort of thing was usually done to houses where the reaction would be known beforehand. It seemed that dust buckets spent a lot of time outside. They were mostly filled with ashes and were often the wrong way up.

For those old enough to be allowed in, the Mission was the Mecca of all boys. If you were there and under age someone would report you and out you would have to go. Boys started their billiards by booking up for a quarter of an hour on the small table. From there they progressed to the big table, and snooker as well. The magic word in the Mission was Tournament. On the night of the final everyone crept around, hardly daring to breathe. Beside games there was a set of books about the first world war, which were always being looked at. The large coal fire with chairs around it was always popular in winter and the familiar faces would be in position each evening. It took a war to make dramatic changes there. A canteen was built to serve the great number of servicemen stationed in the town. Bathrooms were added and used by servicemen and by residents without this facility. Bedrooms were also added for any shipwrecked sailors.

When the Mission was closed the youngsters of the town lost a place of sport, refreshment, relaxation and worship. The town also lost the services of the Port Missioner, the office that the late Mr. M.L.Hawken had carried out as adviser, friend and preacher for so many years.

WE July 1926 St. Ives Town Council, Highway Committee. The Surveyor reported the receipt of a letter *signed by various persons objecting to the making good of the street known as The Ropewalk near the Island, and the Committee, in view of the circumstances surrounding the street, recommended the Council not to proceed with the work.*

The Breakwater, Viadock and Rampers

There was no finer playground in all St. Ives than the area known as the Breakwater. First and foremost it was the place where all the town's rubbish was formerly dumped. Any requirement could be found there from iron bedsteads for the camp to pieces of hoop iron for corken barbers and tins for making boats. Of course this treasure trove was not restricted to boys alone, and many a problem had been solved by something "found down breakwater". In addition there were pig scrows, pigeon lofts, discarded boats, bark houses, as well as building and repairs to fishing boats. Chicken had free range facilities. This area has now become the Porthgwidden car park. Much of the space was formed by the quarrying of rock to build the breakwater which was commenced in 1817 from Bamaluz point, and for the infilling of the wooden piles which extended from the stone New Pier in 1864. The term Breakwater College is still used in a light hearted way when listing one's educational background. With so much activity it must have been a seat of much knowledge and experience of life.

The wooden piles extending from the New Pier, although getting fewer as the years went by, were always referred to as The Rampers, although it was a breakwater, and three tiers of fishing boats had moorings between it and the back of Smeaton's Pier before the extension was commenced in 1888. It had its own light on the extreme end, tended by a lady who walked the length of it on a plank. In spite of all that, it never took away the name Breakwater from its predecessor.

The sand between the Breakwater and the New Pier was

known as The Viadock. Exactly why this should be is not clear, perhaps there was some sort of viaduct erected to bring stone across for building the New Pier, but this has been lost in time. Confusion could sometimes arise over the use of the words New Pier and New Quay, after the West Pier was built in 1894. Not many towns have two piers referred to as New when the newest is almost a hundred years old. The Downlong division shows itself here, as one always goes up the New Quay (West Pier) but down the other pier.

The building of a breakwater at St. Ives and making the bay a harbour of refuge has been discussed for at least 150 years, and was always on the election address of every candidate that ever stood in the town elections. Many times it came very close to realisation, even after the second world war efforts were made to use part of a Mulberry harbour, but the bay is still empty. During the 1930's when there were hard times in the town the Mayor made an appeal to businessmen to subscribe weekly to his fund to give work to unemployed men to build a concrete groin at the inner end of the Rampers, that would serve as a half-tide breakwater.

May 1937 A meeting of the Mayor's Unemployment Fund Committee held at the Bay View Lodge. Mr. C.S.Prynne (Hon.Sec.) said the total amount subscribed to the 6th May was £276.2s.11d. and up to last Saturday 42 men had been employed.The work consisted of replacing stone set in concrete. At present the work has extended for a length of 57 feet by 30 feet wide and 6 feet in height, making a solid block of 380 cubic yards. It was decided to close the Fund from 10th June and a fresh appeal made on 1st October that work might proceed next winter.

Picking up coal

Any event in the harbour was of interest to boys. The one showing the most profit was the arrival of any ship loaded with coal for the gasworks or the local coal merchants.

During the 1930's there were still a few sailing vessels about as well as the steamers which were also being replaced with motor craft, and these were usually Dutch.

Local dockers with long handled shovels would shovel the coal into baskets. These were hoisted by winch, two at a time, to the level of the cart or lorry. Two men would grab the baskets and tip them into the vehicle until a mound arose to a safe height.

The journey to the gasworks at Porthmeor or coal stores at the Digey, Island Road or the Back Roads was followed by boys with their buckets, awaiting the pieces of coal as they fell off. Iron rimmed cart wheels on cobbles are ideal for disturbing the load, and the large stones put on the corners of many Downlong houses to protect the house were safe bets for a cascade of coal when struck by a wheel. For carts wishing to mount Dicks Hill, ponies were tied to the bollard beside the Shamrock Lodge. The sudden jerk as the two animals took the strain to mount the hill was always good for a few pieces and the changing of gear on a lorry often had the same effect. A piece of wood or a stone placed in front of a cart wheel was often one of the tricks tried, but at no time was coal taken other than that which fell. This was not only a schoolboy hobby, as a good spillage soon brought out the nearest householder with shovel and bucket.

It was possible to buy a cartload of coal straight from the quayside. This was tipped outside the house, to be carried into the coal cellar or under the stairs, which is where most houses kept their coal.

At the close of the day's work the completely black dockers would be seen walking home to clean themselves in houses which had no bathrooms or hot water except for kettles boiled on the slab. These men worked very hard, as being a tidal harbour a delay in catching the tide would mean another 12 hours before departure of the ship.

The departure of any kind of coal boat was always of interest, steam being the most spectacular. With a local pilot on the bridge the ship would go astern until a single wire rope checked her way, then slowly coming ahead and, clearing the pier head, the pilot would descend the ship's ladder to the waiting skiff or the pilot boat *Ada* which would often then take the pilot to another ship waiting entrance to the harbour or to enter Hayle. For those with the opportunity there was a miniature coal mine waiting on the sand where the craft had discharged. As soon as the tide had eased this area was then cleared, not always by boys, as some men were also waiting for the black diamonds.

The wreck of the *Alba* on the Island rocks in January 1938 brought a coal mine to the rocks at Porthmeor. Much of the cargo of coal was salvaged but some found its way among the rocks and eventually fireplaces in the town. Unfortunately the coal was of the steam variety and not household coal. It was very difficult to light but would burn amongst other coal. This coal was found for quite a few years. Movement of sand among the rocks would disclose more coal which had been rounded by the action of the sea.

SWS 1889 Mr. J.Daniel, Coal Merchant, had coal stores in Shute Street (Street- an- Pol) and in Fore Street. Mr. Warren would discharge best Red Ash coal from the vessel *Willie* straight from the quay to your home for the cash price of 22s.0d. per ton.

WE During the first world war coal was controlled in price by the Household Fuel and Lighting Order and a price rise was announced to take effect from 17th March 1920.

Railborne		Seaborne	
per ton delivered	54/2	per ton delivered	60/2
per ton at depot	50/4	per ton at depot	56/4
per cwt delivered	2/9	per cwt delivered	2/11
per cwt at depot	2/7	per cwt at depot	2/9

WE 1920 The coal strike in October caused an emergency order to be passed that only one cwt of coal per house, per week, was allowed and none whatever to those who had half a ton in their possession.

In May 1921 after another coal strike had lasted five weeks the situation at St. Ives was serious, as many houses were without coal. The truck load that had arrived at St. Ives station was disposed of in small quantities by the authorities at 4s.5d. per cwt, so it is doubtful that much went below the Market House. The Corporation gasworks also had to cut its supply, gas being available from 7 am to 9 am, 11 am to 1.30 pm and 4.30 pm to 10.30 pm only. The steamers that were trading to Hayle had to take in wood and coke owing to the scarcity of bunker coal.

In July the local Emergency Committee purchased 40 tons of Saar Valley coal which was offered for sale at 6s.8d. per cwt.

In August there was the welcome sight of the *S.S.Abercraig* discharging a cargo of coal in St. Ives for Messrs. J.Daniel & Sons. It was indeed fortunate that the strike was in the summer months, but with no electricity, and gas restricted, many must have had to rely on neighbours and friends for their washing and cooking, and no doubt a lot of wood was turned into ash during the 89 day stoppage. The General Strike of 1926 commenced with 300 tons of coal at St. Ives and the *S.S.Stanwell* arrived in the bay with a further cargo. A Coal Committee was formed consisting of Messrs. W.Hollow, C.Lander, M.Stevens, E.Daniel, J.Daniel, S.C.Beckerleg, with Lewis Richards as Coal Officer.

In October the Fishermen's Co-operative Society was still selling coal at 3s.4d. per cwt. Cheap coal would be the greatest boon in the fishermens' houses, where the only means of cooking was by the slab. This price was cheap compared with 4s.2d. at other yards.

WE November 1921 The Coal Committee issued a notice from 5th November:-

A. To increase the domestic coal ration from one cwt to two cwt per fortnight.

B. To bring coke under the rationing and permit system.

C. To forbid the purchase of coal without a permit.

The rule is still in force that says "No further coal may be acquired as long as the householder has 5 cwt in stock".

WE December 1926 *The price of coal in St. Ives went down from 4s.4d. to 4s.0d. per cwt delivered, and from 4s.2d. to 3s.10d. at the yard. Then in the Christmas week the price came down again from 3s.6d. to 3s.4d. per cwt.*

P.C. Keast, who had for the past month been on duty in the coalfields, now returned to his duties at St. Ives.

With electricity cable being laid down through Tregenna Hill, the reliance on coal had gone, as far as a part of St. Ives was concerned.

Fishing

With fishing being in the blood it was only natural for it to be one of the favourite pastimes in the rock pools at the back of the Island. Fish of the blenny family lived there under the rocks. Mulley was the local name for them, but there were other variations known as darkies and on occasions some whistle fish.

A piece of cotton and a bent pin were often used, but to fish properly it would be best to get fly-hooks at five for a halfpenny at the Co-op in Wharf Road, but half-pennies were scarce.

The best bait was obtained by knocking a limpet (locally a lempot) from the rock with a stone, then, pressing the belly of the fish, a black section would appear which was fixed to the hook. To catch crabs the rest of the limpet was used. The fish were always put back into the pools again as we had all learned from experience that fish would not live overnight in a jam jar.

From rock pool fishing it was only a short step to sea fishing. A line of five or six hooks to catch 'flukes' from the quay, or boats moored across the harbour, soon turned into a tackle of 25 hooks to be placed in position on the Cock Bank or taken to some other favourable spot in a punt, to be recovered a few hours later.

Bass fishing on 'Meor beach was done with slate tackle. A piece of slate from an old roof would be drilled in the middle with a nail. A stout piece of skiliven known as an orsell was threaded through and knotted. A lighter piece of line with a hook was then affixed to the orsell. Pits were dug in the sand about four feet apart, and a slate placed in each. These were filled in and a line of hooks would then stretch across the sand according to the number one wished to use. Twenty five was a reasonable number for one person. If the height of the tide was falling care had to be taken not to set these slates too far out in case they were beyond reach at the next low water. Except when fishing for mackerel from a boat using a metal spinner it was necessary to obtain bait. Lugworms were dug in the harbour, making sure to backfill the pits before the Harbour Master came on the scene.

If a boat had been drawing for bait there were often enough linces to be found under her bottom boards to meet all needs. The alternative was to scrape for your own. A vindler would be made by a blacksmith for a few pence, or a bread knife could be adapted. The best places to scrape for bait were where the sewer water left the pipe either at Porthmeor or at the back of the West Pier. This polluted water caused the linces to give themselves up, which saved a lot of scraping.

The best fishing was for whiting during November and December. This was a busy time as the herring season would be in full swing. As soon as the end of Smeaton's Pier was clear of boats every vantage point had an angler, especially on the steps and under the lights. These were all hand lines, there being no rod fishing in St. Ives at this time.

The whiting were big enough to eat, but not big fish like those being caught in the bay on hand lines from the boats riding at their nets. The West Pier was fished by more elderly gentlemen. Regardless of the quantity of fish caught there was always someone coming along with news that we ought to see what they were catching on the other pier.

For bait we used a piece of pilchard or herring but after

catching one whiting this could then be used for the rest of the time.

The Harbour

As soon as a boy was big enough to look after himself he was taught to scull a punt. If his father owned a boat the punt was always available and this opened up a new world to a boy. Not only was he able to give men a shove aboard or a shove ashore, but there was a whole bay for fishing or pleasure trips. After mastering the art of sculling with two hands there were other variations such as two on one oar with one boy standing on the thwart, sitting down, and sculling with one hand.

The ability to get about opened up new places to shoot tackle and to fish with a line. With a favourable wind, after sculling out for some distance, a make- shift sail of bottom boards was erected for a sail back into the harbour.

An essential requirement for playing in the harbour was the ability to climb the ladder near the arches. The ladder has been replaced in recent years and now seems easier to climb, but the top rung of the old ladder seemed a long way down to little boys and the length of chain with a ring which was at the top was more hindrance than help. It was certainly a feather in one's cap to be able to negotiate this ladder in safety.

Perhaps it should be mentioned that the sand in the harbour was never used for pleasure except by children, as the sand was not as clean as in recent years. It was just a working surface. One of the things going on in the summer was the skinning of dog fish. Wooden benches with a top bar with iron hooks were placed on the sand, and men and women were engaged to skin and clean dogfish for consumption further up the line. These fish were sold very cheaply and were the kind of fish that were often dumped and never sold and eaten locally. Known as flake it became rock salmon further up the country.

With fish offal and dead fish along the tide marks there

were many gulls around the harbour, but at dusk each evening all the gulls went west to their nesting sites on the western shores. There was no nesting among the roofs or chimneys of the town. A sea bird which used to provoke a song was a Kidda, Jack Cocking or guillemot. Children would sing to it to make it dive: "Jack Cocking go under, salt water, dry land". Although the song is difficult to understand the birds used to dive just the same.

In summer there were often boys swimming around the inner quay steps, diving from the steps, the rail, or from the lamp post, according to ability. Cherrying, the art of swimming under water, was much practiced, and, on request, the "porpoise dive" was performed for admiring onlookers.

With so much rubbish being thrown into the sea or on the rocks at the Breakwater, which was the town refuse dump for a number of years, there were always plenty of slates about, and the skimming of slates across the top of the water was entered into with much enthusiasm. If a ball had gone into the sea much stone throwing was encouraged to try to knock the ball into a place from where it could be recovered. This same method was also used to recover wayward corken barbers, often with disastrous results to the boat.

For the very brave, or the very foolish, there was a ledge at the back of the quay, about eight inches wide. To walk along it towards the middle lighthouse was considered quite a feat, but for the less adventurous there was always the harbour junk, the 13 inch manilla rope which was used to secure steamers to the quayside. The aim in both cases was to walk its length without falling off.

On some days there would be some type of stall at the top of the slipway. One demonstration was of two packets of cigarettes held under water in a glass bowl. On opening the packets it was always the Kensitas which were dry, the wet ones were thrown onto the sand, to be recovered and dried by the boys. Near the top of the slipway a large pipe often poured floodwater onto the sand. This pipe had a hinged iron cover and when this was opened it could be closed with quite a bang, giving a fright to unsuspecting passers- by.

The launching of a new boat would mean providing a bottle of pop and buns for the children, but there were more boats being sold than being launched during the 1930's.

The harbour scene was enlivened during the mid 30's by the arrival of Sir Oswald Mosley's Blackshirts. One of the boats became their headquarters and many lively meetings were held on the harbour front.

Smeaton's Pier was at first only a short pier of 320 feet, built between 1766 and 1770. The four sided stone lighthouse was built in 1831, 60 years later. This was lit by candles or oil and then with the building of the gas works it was thereafter lit by gas. The 280 foot Victorian extension was completed in 1890, the new lighthouse first being lit on the 2nd September, three months after the official opening of the quay. The fixed red sector showing from shore to the New Pier buoy, a green sector showing at less than 10 feet of water at the pier head, and showing white at more than 10 feet. Up to the war years a glass slide was manually moved by a local keeper, which meant going down to the lighthouse at least twice a night, sometimes more. After the war electric electrodes were installed to make the changes automatic.

WE August 1933 Here and there -Wayfarer.

A correspondent shows great interest in the Wharf Road, but is apparently under mistaken impressions. He refers to a "Little thing by the Wharf" and wants to know whether it is to hold refuse from the cafes or to be used as a perambulator park. I have the doubtful honour to inform him that the structure is intended to fulfil the duties of a bandstand, and it is actually called (by those who possess great imaginative powers) a bandstand.

WE October 1934 Blackshirts return visit.

A further meeting was held on Friday night. A crowd of 1,000 attended, but from the start they adopted a hostile

*attitude. Fireworks were let off and the speakers bombard-
ed with seaweed. The police advised the speakers to end
their meeting and the van drove off.*

WE November 1935 *Four Blackshirts had a meeting in
Market Strand on Saturday evening. The hecklers were
dominant to such an extent that many could not hear anything worth repeating. The listeners crept out into the
roadway making it exceedingly awkward for traffic
approaching or leaving the Wharf Road or West Pier.
There was no repetition of the scenes witnessed a year ago
when the Blackshirts paid their first visit to St. Ives.*

WE July 1945 *Resignation of Light Keeper. Mr. James
Cocking has resigned his position after 30 years service.*

On the 8th October 1979 the red, green and white lights
were replaced by two green lights, one six feet above the
other. The blue light on the West Pier was replaced by two
red lights. This was done on the instructions of the Trinity
House, when all UK harbour lights became standard.

Seasons

There is no such thing as a paid holiday for a share fisherman. Whilst other people were coming to the town on holiday we had never heard of any of the fishing community
going away for a holiday or a honeymoon. Men were mar-
ried on Saturday or Sunday and were at sea on Monday.

The year was divided into seasons or tracks. Fish did
not come every day of the year, indeed they might not
come at all. When our fathers were youths there had been
a spring mackerel season and an Irish and North Sea herring fishery. After the end of the first world war, with the
release of the steam trawlers from mine sweeping duties,
these seasons ceased to be, the last boats that went to the
North Sea failed to cover their expenses entailed in bark-
ing, coaling and provisions for the trip. The men spent the
months of January and February in the net lofts mending
the herring nets. Nets were also mended in the home as
well as the making of new crab nets. Wire crab pots were

also made and repaired in the lofts by those intending to fish for shellfish in the Summer season.

During this period of repair and preparation there was no money being earned, and how people could afford to live is one of the mysteries of life, but the children always had a meal.

The first season of the year was the lining season. This only involved half a dozen big boats. The start depended on the weather. This was usually February or March, with every effort to fish during Easter week when prices were higher.

The right ground in which to shoot the lines, which stretched for eight or nine miles with 5,000 hooks, had been discovered over the years. Commencing at 18 miles it reached to over 80 miles when fishing ceased to be a paying proposition.

Boats usually went to sea on Monday, Wednesday and Friday, landing on the following day, extra bait and ice sometimes extending the trip another day, with the weather, parting of gear and failure of engine and hauling winch throwing all schedules haywire. The bait used was mackerel or pilchard, but those boats that had a lincey net caught their own sand eel bait before the day's work began in earnest.

The rest of the boats had got their tiers of crab pots and nets ready, and were awaiting fine weather in which to pursue their fishery. Old pots and nets were used in April whilst there was the chance of a ground swell destroying gear so early in the season. Pots were baited with red ellick or mackerel. Any fish caught were stored in store pots at the back of Smeaton's Pier or off Porthminster. Depending on the amount of fish the season lasted from April until the end of August. A handful of boats also favoured the trawl and fished the bay, western shore line, or along the shores of Bassetts Bay.

It depended on what gear the boat owner had in his loft as to what season he was engaged on. Like all business men, fishermen were always listening for news of better prospects on other shores and the news of pilchards in Mounts Bay was the signal for boats of all sizes to prepare to go around land for this season, which was always a precarious one. It usually started in July but often had a premature ending.

The one season in which every size of boat took part was the St. Ives Bay herring season. Fish do not stick to calendar dates but November to the end of December with plenty of blanks in between was the expected season. The bigger boats followed the shoals around land to Plymouth, but all were back and gear safely in the loft and boats in Lelant, before the end of January. The earnings from this season were to feed and clothe the family until the Spring or even summer. The failure of the herring season meant great distress in the town, and with each season showing a decline, men were looking to other lands in which to earn a living.

Some small boats and pleasure boats caught mackerel during the summer months. This entailed towing a line with a three pound lead and a spinner, with the hope of catching one fish at a time. This was a slow way of catching fish which was changed during the second world war when a Scottish sailor stationed at St. Ives introduced a method of catching fish in great numbers by the use of feather lures attached to a string of hooks, and in so doing changed the whole fishery.

Most of the Whiffers, as the boats were called, also had other occupations during the day, the mackerel being caught mostly at early morning or evening and not regarded as a season. The fish compared unfavourably with those caught by net in the former spring mackerel season.

Some seasons overlapped each other and decisions had to be made as to which track was the best to be on. The re-appearance of fish sometimes entailed re-loading nets and gear which it was thought had been finished with until another year.

The Watchers

During the longline fishing season it was the custom of boys whose fathers were still at sea and due to come to land around that time, to go to the church on the Island to watch for the first sign of a boat on the horizon. In former days when there had been a large fleet boys were rewarded with a "penny for news" when boats were sighted and reported. We had fewer boats to choose from, but were proud of our ability to pick out certain boats whilst still just a dot, and well before it was obvious to all which boat it was.

If it was the one we were looking for we then spread the news to all who were interested, and if it was the *Sheerness* we were often rewarded with a sweet from the little shop in Quay Street.

4 PILCHARDS AND HERRING

The pilchard season

Although living in a town which owed its prosperity to the humble pilchard, I cannot remember any "pilcher" season at St. Ives.

For boats with pilchard nets the months of June to September were spent at Newlyn. It was always a troubled season with gluts and price disputes causing the unexpected return of men at any time. The season started with the doubtful privilege of a trip "around the land" and a "shoot" near the Wolf lighthouse, with the eventual arrival at Newlyn. This was considered to be a treat for the boys, which many of us failed to appreciate.

The pilchard was a "poor peoples" fish, eaten chiefly in Italy, there being no other market with English shops selling tinned pilchards from abroad. The buyers usually had their own agreed boats and price. The men counted their own fish, handling six fish at a time with 126 to the hundred.

At the end of the season most of the mending was done in the net lofts, as the curing by creosote (pickle) made them too dirty and strong smelling to mend in the house. In earlier days the men used to sleep in the Newlyn net lofts, but improved cabin accommodation made this unnecessary.

In chasing the fish shoals, it was often necessary to work near the Wolf lighthouse, in what was known as the steamboat tracks. This often resulted in damage or loss of nets, as ships ploughed through the fleet. On Mondays and Saturdays the men were transported to and from St. Ives Malakoff and Newlyn quay, but times had been so hard that the men walked home, not having earned enough to pay their bus or train fare.

WE September 1889 Pickling has practically limited the quantity of pilchards which will be exported from our shores at present. When fish were bulked immense quantities could be saved as the bulks could be built long and high, but now, Presto! all this changed and a fish cellar is only capable of furnishing about one fifth of the accommodation for tanked fish it could supply for bulk.

Pilchard seine fishing. The total number of seines represented on the St. Ives fishery this year will be 164. This number is two seines less than last year.

WE November 1889 *Hevva! The welcome sound of Hevva! was heard at St. Ives on Wednesday, two seines were shot. The Bolitho Co. have secured about 600 hogsheads and the Cornwall Co. about 70 hogsheads.*

On Thursday morning boat loads of fish were brought in and carted to the cellars. As the fish are being pickled very few hands are employed in curing them.

WE January 1899 *Property for sale. All those leasehold fish cellars and seine lofts known as Flamank's Court, situated partly in the Digey and partly in Flamank's Court.*

WE July 1920 *Meeting of Cornwall Sea Fisheries Committee. The curers deemed 20/- per thousand the utmost that could be paid for pilchards during the present season. Consequently, the proposition for the catcher was either to abandon the pilchard fishery or seek some outside assistance. Most of the material used by the fishermen had risen 500 to 600% in price, yet 20/- per thousand was the same price as we got in 1914. A white net could previously be purchased for £2.10s., today it costs £14 or £15. The pre-war price of fuel oil was 6d. per gallon, now it was offered in some cases for 2/-.*

One of the best boats last year did average above 10,700 pilchards per week the whole season. Now it was estimated that a large boat must catch 10,000 weekly at 20/- per thousand to pay expenses only in fuel, lubricating oil, groceries and coal. These specified items were recognised costs of working a boat and were deducted prior to the men dividing their earnings into their respective shares.

WE April 1921 *SEINE BOATS AT PORTHMINSTER.*

Cornwall Fishery Company to be asked by the Council to remove seine boats from the Boat Plot at Porthminster. These boats had not brought any revenue to the town for the past nine years and they are now an eyesore.

WE September 1921 *THE MOUNTS BAY PILCHARD FISHERY. Most of the St. Ives boats engaged in the pilchard fishery round land have returned and we are sorry to record that the season has proved unremunerative.*

WE July 1922 *SLUMP IN PILCHARDS. A conference of representative merchants of Mousehole, Newlyn, Porthleven, St. Ives and ports east of the Lizard, held at Newlyn to determine the prices to be paid to fishermen engaged in the Mounts Bay and Western Drift pilchard fishery during the next three or four months, decided to commence the season by giving the catcher 15/- per thousand.*

It was observed that from the 1921 season there were still 16,000 barrels of pilchards unsold in this country and in Mediterranean ports. Practically throughout the past season the main fleet of Mounts Bay and St. Ives drifters were forced to shoot their trains in very deep grounds in the vicinity of the Wolf lighthouse, which necessitated the consumption of large quantities of oil and heavy motoring expenses, the price of 25/- to 30/- per 1000 leaving the barest margin for sharing.

WE July 1922 *ROUND THE TOWN, by Observer. If the pilchards are not worth more than 15/- per thousand, are the carters, cellarmen and women, and other people employed in the curing to have the same wages as last year, when pilchards brought more money? It is certainly unfair that everybody concerned should make a better living out of fish than the fishermen.*

WE August 1922 *The exporters and merchants concerned in the pilchard industry have decided the 15/- per thousand for pilchards is totally inadequate. The Conference decided to advance the price to 22/6 per thousand.*

Daily Mail September 1922 *WATCHING FOR*

PILCHARDS. Perched high above a precipitous cliff at St. Ives is a tiny snow white cottage. In it dwell two old fishermen, William Bryant Noall and Edward Cothey, and from dawn to sunset they keep a lookout. Day by day for 14 years they have kept their watch. They look and long for the return of the pilchard. Fourteen years ago there was the greatest catch ever known; since then the pilchard has disappeared.

***WE September 1923** For the first time in living memory (1776) no seiners are in pay at St. Ives for the pilchard season. It is regrettable that such an interesting old fishery has died out, but apparently it was inevitable.*

***WE September 1926** Pilchards have been seen in very large numbers quite close to St. Ives and many thousands have been caught in waters nearer St. Ives than to Newlyn. Therefore why have our men to go to Newlyn and remain away from their homes each week when there are still available large fish cellars in St. Ives, and tanks whose total capacity far exceeds those in Newlyn? The answer is that there are at present no buyers of pilchards in St. Ives. For many years St. Ives was the most famous place in the world for the pilchard fishery.*

***WE January 1928** THE LAST OF THE OLD SEINE BOATS AT PORTHMINSTER. The extinction of an important St. Ives industry has been rendered complete recently by the removal of the last of the old seine boats from Porthminster Green. Less than 40 years ago St. Ives pilchard seine fishery gave employment to at least 200 to 300 fishermen and when the cry of "Hevva" was heard hundreds more dropped their work to run and help in securing the shoal of fish. Gradually the old seine boats have been disappearing, and now the last has gone.*

***WE September 1929** GLUT OF PILCHARDS. PRACTICALLY ALL THE CURERS TANKS FILLED. A remarkable situation in the Cornish pilchard fishery arose on Monday by the refusal of the fishermen at Newlyn to go to sea on account of the big drop in prices offered by buyers. Thirty five boats from St. Ives have been fishing in Newlyn*

Newlyn since the 1st of July. The price paid was 25/- per thousand. This was later increased to £2, but at that time there was very light fishing. Since then, however, the price was rapidly reduced to £1, this being paid for the past two weeks. Most St. Ives men were willing to fish for this, but on Monday they were informed the price would be cut to 15/-. This was considered absolutely inadequate, and consequently with men from Looe and Mevagissey, the St. Ives men declined to put to sea and returned to their home port.

WE *August 1932 FIRST HALF OF CORNISH SEASON DISAPPOINTING. The fleets were increased last week to over 70 drifters. Owing to inclement weather the small craft shot in Mounts Bay on most nights, but meshings were insufficient to command a sale. Larger boats ventured to within a few miles of the Wolf, combined landings for five nights trials were computed at 405,000. Prices for curing were, 12/6 - 15/- per 1000, local longliners and jousters were supplied at 2/- to 3/- per 126.*

WE September 1932 *NEWLYN FISHERY STRIKE. FISH-ERMEN REFUSE TO GO TO SEA. During the greater part of the season the price has been 15/- per thousand. During last weekend one or two merchants decided to bring the price down to 12/6 per thousand. On Monday when this was known, the crews who fished for these buyers refused to put to sea and about 30 boats, mostly from St. Ives, Looe and Fowey, remained in harbour.*

WE September 1933 *HUGE CATCH OF PILCHARDS. ENORMOUS LOSS OF NETS. Three million pilchards , the largest catch for half a century, were landed in Mounts Bay on Thursday. The **Sheerness**, which netted 8 to 9 lasts (about 90,000 fish), was packed from mast to mast, although she is the largest boat in the local fleet. Unfortunately, this enormous haul, which should have done much to relieve the depression in the industry, was accompanied by the loss of over 100 nets, valued at £500 to £600. These losses were caused, ironically enough, by the weight of the fish, for the nets were dragged to the bot-*

tom of the sea. St. Ives boat losses: **Our John** 17 nets of 100 yards, valued £102, **Maggie** 16 nets £96, **Ripple** 8 nets £48. This is the most serious loss that the West Cornwall boats have suffered for many years. The huge catches will not compensate for the loss of nets. Prices for best fish were maintained at 15/- per thousand.

WE April 1936 RESULT OF IMPOSITION OF SANCTIONS. A Western Morning News representative met three English exporters at Newlyn on Tuesday, at their request, in order that publicity might be given to the matter. They told him that pilchards exported by English firms were being refused landing in Italy, and as a result they had cellars filled with cured pilchards for which they could find no market.

WE June 1936 ST. IVES FISHING BOAT'S LOSSES. The **Queen Mary** entering the English Channel on Wednesday morning on her return from America, is believed to have ripped away five nets belonging to the St. Ives fishing boat **Excellent**, fishing 25 miles SSW of Mousehole when at 3 a.m. a liner appeared out of thick fog and tore away the nets. Members of the crew said she was unmistakably the **Queen Mary**. About half a mile of nets separated the liner from the fishing craft. The loss of nets was a serious matter, but the crew were relieved that the liner did not come any nearer.

WE September 1938 Fishing for pilchards off the Wolf Rock the St. Ives fishing boat **Sheerness** landed the highest catch of the season, at Newlyn, of 94,000 pilchards. Because of the risk involved in the Italian market, Newlyn fish buyers reduced the price paid for pilchards from 15/- to 10/- per thousand. Fishermen from Mevagissey, Polperro, Looe and St. Ives, feeling this return is inadequate for them to make a living, did not put to sea, and some have since returned to their home ports. Newlyn and Mousehole boats number about 15 out of a fleet of 60 and were the only boats to put to sea.

The herring season

The coming of the winter herring season was an event looked forward to by young and old alike, always hoping that it would be better than last year, when fishing had been slight or the fish in "lucky bags". In other words, one boat having a good catch but other boats shooting their nets almost alongside had "black nets" coming in the same as they went out.

The majority of fishermen had been watching the results of the small fry who had been trying close inshore with four or five nets, on the theory that the larger boats with larger fleets of nets should catch more fish. A gurry of herrings caught off Porthminster would be enough to waken the town. Probably for some weeks the small boats had been the focus of attention, with most of them in by 8 pm. Men had been on the pier and by the Lodges awaiting their arrival, not daring to go home until the last boat had returned, in case the fish had arrived.

The first gurry of herrings was the signal for the town to become alive with feverish activity the next morning. Flat carts loaded with nets went down to the boats from the lofts or bark houses. If the sea was in the harbour the boats would be moving to the quay to load, tins of paraffin going on board, and everyone with an interest in the fishing would have a job to do. No doubt the Scotch girls were already prepared in the kipper houses and more barrels would be piled up on the Wharf Road. In the homes the oilskin frocks had already dried after their coat of oil and a tin or a frail had been made ready for foodstuff to be taken aboard. Hessian aprons known as soggets were also ready for the women to wear when counting the fish.

As school children, our part in this was only to see the activity as we went to school in the morning, and saw the work still going on at dinner-time. Our great time came at 4 o'clock when the school was over, reporting home first, then running down to the end of Smeaton's pier to see the fleet of around forty boats going out. If the tide was suitable for the fleet to go away almost together, the boats passed the quay almost touching each other. If the sea was flowing in they went away in two's and three's as they floated. Of course if the sea was completely out we would have little to see, as the boats would be at anchor in the roadstead. All the boats were known to us, not always the boat's name or a previous name, sometimes it would be the name of the owner, or a nickname.

With sea breaking on the "rudge" the boats' bows would shoot into the air, coming down with such a shock that the engine would often have to be restarted.

Some of the fleet such as the *Gratitude* and *Young John* had helped to make up the fleet of boats that had fished the North Sea under sail before the first war. *Barnabas* and *Humility* had sailed for herring before the motors had been installed. The "Blue" gigs, *Our Girls* and *Thrive*, had been built in the town or on the harbour sand, then the clinker gigs *Daisy* and *Diana* which had worked the bay under oars in earlier days. Each boat represented five or six men who were looking for a clear space in the bay where they might obtain a night's work to provide for their families.

As soon as the dark had descended the whole bay became a town of bobbing lights, a sight which will never be repeated. Some boats had electric lights, others had carbide. Many had paraffin lamps, while a few had searchlights which was quite a novelty. With each boat having a light at the masthead which bobbed and waved as the boats rocked, and the deck lights being occasionally hidden as the men went about their work, the bay was a mass of flashing lights.

On shore the whole scene was watched with interest by the men on the Castle or the top of the quay. Most boats were known by their lights and any movement was watched and interpreted by those ashore who had been through it all before.

As soon as the first boat was seen making for the harbour the drift of men towards the pier head commenced. If fishing was light the nets would appear clean. Fish all over the deck and in the nets was a good sign, but the depth of the boat in the water was the main indication of the amount of fish on board. Within three hours the majority of the fleet would be back in harbour, but depending on the weather, state of the tide or previous fish movements, some boats would stay out to try their luck again.

For those at home during the evening the first intimation of the returning fleet would be the clump of leather, or the quieter sound of rubber, sea boots passing by. The lateness of men coming in might well indicate a few fish caught, but to be covered in shales (scales) and the request for the kettle to be put on might well indicate a return to the boats to unmesh 8 or 10 gurries as a rough estimate.

Apart from Saturday mornings and the Christmas holiday period, as children we missed the activity in the harbour and on the foreshore. There being enough fish to require the wives down to count, usually two gurries were brought to the chosen spot, baskets of herring were then brought by horse and cart and tipped into the gurries. With one woman at each end, and the Skipper's wife to keep the score, the fish were then counted into the buyers' barrels. Picking up the fish in threes, which was known as a cast, the audible count reached 40 with another cast acknowledged by the scorekeeper. The hundred of herring which was worth 123 was recorded in the notebook with one stroke, and after four strokes the fifth was across like a gate. For doing this work the women were rewarded with a little 'lowance (allowance) which varied with different boats.

A gurry was a wooden box with shafts at each end, and depending on the size of the fish it held about 800 herring. At one period men were employed as gurry carriers, and with the help of a shoulder harness they would carry the fish from the boats up across the sand to the women waiting at the Wharf. In counting fish the numbers were called in reverse, e.g. six and twenty, seven and twenty etc. until 40 was reached and the call "score Ma" completed the hundred with an extra cast to make it 123. No doubt the extra 23 was to compensate for damaged fish, but the amount for the hundred varied with different ports.

The herring season from October to Christmas was not bound to any set times, but in January the bigger boats would be prepared to go around land to Mounts Bay, following the shoals to Mevagissey and finally to Plymouth. At the close of the season the nets were spread on the Island to dry, then safely stored in the net lofts. Each net would then have to be overhauled, and every broken mesh and hole repaired by men and women either in the loft or at home.

SWS November 1889 On Monday night and Tuesday morning extraordinary catches of herrings were landed, some of the boats had so much fish that the men were obliged to cut away their nets. The highest catch was about 50,000. Those living in Fore Street had very little rest on Tuesday as the carts were running all night. About 300 tons of fish were despatched by rail on Tuesday, and one boat sailed for Swansea with 50,000 herrings to try to make a better price as they were selling at St. Ives as low as 6d a 120.

SWS October 1890 Our boats have been trying for herrings for several nights, but with little success. A movement is on foot to try to put a stop to Saturday night's and Monday morning's fishing. About 500 fishermen have expressed their readiness not to do so. They believe it will be much better for all concerned, as the rest on Saturday night will put a stop to Sunday labour and will have a tendency to clear the markets, thereby giving the chance of a better price for fish sent in the early part of the week.

SWS November 1890 On Thursday over 650 telegrams were received and despatched from St. Ives Post Office. Today, Friday, there are again immense catches, and it is estimated that in four days over 1,000 tons of fish have been despatched from St. Ives station. The fish carts on Friday lined the road from the station to the Summary office in Fore Street.

SWS November 1899 Quite a large number of Newlyn

fishermen arrived at St. Ives on Monday to engage in the herring fishery. About 150 Mousehole and Newlyn men have been engaged.

SWS November 1901 *There are about 140 boats engaged in the herring fishery. Owing to the prevalence of a large number of dog fish in the Bay, the herrings not only disappeared but considerable damage was done to the nets, so much that many fishermen were kept ashore on Wednesday night.*

WE December 1920 *Huge landings by the local fleet. The total catch was estimated to be 200 lasts or 2,000,000 fish, which is the largest quantity landed in one day for 15 years. Several of the boats were deeply laden, and some sustained very heavy losses owing to the weight of the fish. The catches ranged from 70,000 per boat downwards, but unfortunately prices ruled very low, varying from 1/6 to 2/- per hundred. It is estimated that 500 tons of fish were landed, of which 300 tons went by rail to various up-country markets. The remainder were absorbed by the local kippering houses, besides which large quantities were salted in tanks at St. Ives, while motor lorries were running all day conveying fish to Newlyn to be tanked.*

WE August 1921 *Mr. W.E.Shiers, formerly of St. Ives, now of Redruth, thanked the good-hearted fishermen of St. Ives for useful gifts of fish during last winter's fishing. During some weeks he received as much as two boxes a week, which were greatly appreciated by the starving children in Redruth.*

WE December 1921 *Cornwall Sea fisheries. An important point raised was the disparity in the price received by the fishermen and that paid by the consumer, it being contended that the fish purchased by the dealers at 3/- to 4/- a long hundred were retailed at the equivalent of 15/- a hundred or 8 for 1/-.*

WE January 1923 *Herring fishery for the majority of men has been a disastrous one. Not only have fish been scarce but owing to the depredations of dog fish and other causes serious losses of nets have been incurred. The her-*

ring season is usually looked forward to to provide "The winter's bread" but this year many men have scarcely earned anything and the immediate outlook is undoubtedly very serious.

WE February 1923 *NON-PAYMENT OF RATES. Failure of the recent herring fishery resulted in several fishermen being among the defaulters. One fisherman said he only earned £1 during the winter season and lost four nets, and another told the Bench that his total earnings for the season were only 15/-.*

WE January 1924 *CARGO OF HERRINGS. An unusual sight was witnessed at St. Ives on Monday when the steamer* **Edith** *of Liverpool loaded a cargo of herrings for Glasgow. She took in 753 full casks and 933 half casks which we understand are to be despatched to the USA. The fish were cured in the Western Cellars near the Island.*

WE February 1925 *There were over 600 men engaged in the herring fisheries, one half of whom served in the Navy during the Great War. Not one of the men was entitled to any unemployment remuneration or public benefit.*

WE October 1926 *Boxes for the packing of fish are beginning to arrive in preparation for the coming herring season. Small boys have already commenced operations and each night the boxes are disturbed.*

WE December 1926 *The season which opened so promisingly at St. Ives seems likely to end in failure. Last week the results were disappointing and this week has been even worse. During the past few nights ideal weather has prevailed, and the majority of the boats have been at sea, only to return with little or nothing to show as a result of the fishermen's arduous work. Unless there is a speedy improvement the outlook for the winter is dark indeed.*

WE December 1927 *For the large majority it has been a very disappointing season, the effects of which will be keenly felt during the next few months, more especially as last year's Spring mackerel season was such a failure.*

WE December 1928 *Hopes of a good herring season are doomed. Scarcely any herrings have been landed here for* *the week, despite the fact that our men have fished contin-uously from Pendeen to Newquay.*

WE October 1929   *Herrings have arrived.*

"Molicks"

(Fishing air buoys)

From 3/6, each quality guaranteed

J.H.Quick, Sailmaker etc. Victoria Place.

WE November 1929   *Animated scenes have been wit-nessed at St. Ives during the past four weeks where the local fishing fleet are enjoying a splendid harvest. Scenes now being witnessed are reminiscent of the days 20 or 30 years ago, and the whole town is at present a hive of industry. About 80 boats are engaged, employing about 400 men, but in addition to this a similar number are engaged in carting, kippering etc.   About 50 fisher girls have arrived in St. Ives from the North of England. For the first three nights during the present week it is estimated that over 1,100,000 herrings have been landed, prices ranging from 2/3 to 8/9 per 123.*

WE January 1932   *ONE OF THE WORST HERRING SEASONS ON RECORD. With the herring season at Plymouth drawing to a close, this will be remembered as the worst herring season on record as far as Western waters are concerned. During November and December the landings at St. Ives were abnormally low. Since then the majority of our boats have been fishing out of Plymouth with but scant success.*

WE December 1933   *SERIOUS DECLINE OF ST. IVES HERRING FISHERY. We are now within two days of Christmas, when the local fishery usually ends, and only in a few rare instances have our fishermen earned any-thing during the past three months.*

WE December 1933   *The Salvation Army Officers have arranged a dinner for 100 deserving people, and propose opening a soup kitchen during the winter months.   At a meeting of St. Ives Town Council, Councillor Sullivan, referring to the distress in the town, said he had been appalled at its intensity and its extent.*

WE December 1935 A DISAPPOINTING SEASON. The herring season at St. Ives appears to be drawing to a close, and, on the whole, it has been very disappointing. Some good catches were obtained three weeks ago, but with a strong easterly wind the fish disappeared from the coast and since then landings have been light. A few boats are still pursuing the fishery in the Bay, but others have left for Mounts Bay and Plymouth. There were 66 boats, averaging five men in a boat in the St. Ives season.

WE 18 December 1937 SERIOUS PLIGHT OF ST. IVES FISHERMEN. Speaking at a meeting of Cornwall Sea Fisheries Committee at Truro, Mr. W.R.Hollow revealed the fact that 51 St. Ives fishing boats, each having a crew of five or six, have earned only £250 among them this season. Mr. Hollow said that during the last five weeks he had seen St. Ives boats going to sea on nights when it had not been fit for men to be on the water, and they had got nothing for it. How long would the fishery last at this rate? Boys were not going into it, and they could not be blamed. As compared with 51 boats at St. Ives there were 315 forty years ago.

5 FISHING SIDELINES

Smoke houses

A building which was very essential to the fishing industry was a smoke house, often called a kipper house because the type of fish mostly smoked were herring. There were six working during the season, not only for fish caught in St. Ives, but some brought here as well. Just before the herring season began kipper girls came down from Scotland to prepare the houses. No-one knew exactly when the herrings would arrive but everything was prepared.

The smoke, haze and smell of the smoke houses was most welcome as it indicated herring being caught and this would be to everyone's advantage. There was only a limited market for herring and the numbers taken for kippering were a great help to the fishermen. The names Woodger, Holmes, Brown, Pawlyn and Veal were the big smoke houses, with Mr. Carbines doing it in a small way.

SWS 1890 On the completion of the Victoria extension to Smeaton's pier Mr. T.R.Bolitho in his remarks at the pier opening, made the following suggestion; "In regard to the herrings, for which at times sufficient remunerative price cannot be obtained, he would throw out a hint for the consideration of practical men that something may be done in starting a little smoking factory where they could cure their herrings like other people".

That the hint had been taken was shown in an advert from William Veal, Fishmonger, Tregenna Place:

Specialities: Kippers, Bloaters and all kind of cured fish. Fresh kippers and bloaters delivered in time for breakfast.

SWS November 1899 An article on the kipper houses explains that tens of thousands of herring at St.Ives are converted into kippers, bloaters and red herring: "... Scottish girls paid not less then 16/- a week and 25-30,000 are treated per day. After washing in a basket they are drained and remain for some time in strong pickle. Then they go to the pickling house where women and girls earning 8/- a week hang the fish on pegs on two sides of the wooden bars. After draining for some hours they go to the sweating house and from there to the smoke house, some 30 feet high. On the floor are many little heaps of material which will not splutter or burst into flame. Upon opening the door you see nothing but dense light brown smoke. Here the fish are kept for 24 hours. Red herring require four or five weeks, bloaters much less. All boxes are made on the premises - each box contains 30 pair, 60 fish; half a box 15 pair, 30 fish. Up to this time kippering has been a speculation, the supply of herring being inconsistent...".

SWS March 1900 With the outbreak of the South African war, St. Ives fish merchants responded by sending red herring to the troops.

On Saturday, William Veal, fishmerchant, despatched 4,000 selected red herring addressed to the Officer Commanding, D.C.L.I., South Africa. The fish in airtight casks were conveyed by the G.W.R. free to Southampton. Mr. W. Rouncefield, fishmerchant, is also sending five cases to the Cornish Regiment in South Africa. A letter to Mr. Veal from Private James Glasson of Lelant, dated 25th September thanked Mr. Veal for the first fish since arriving in that country.

SWS 1900 Mr. Williams presented plans for a bark house and a smoke house at the old timber yard (now Couch's open car park), and Mr. Carbines had to agree not to light up his fire before 11 pm and to put it out at 4 am in the morning for a smoke house in Fore Street, with the entrance in Virgin Street.

SE December 1940 The advertised sale of smoke house equipment from the Veal family firm marks the end of the industry, no doubt the blackout also contributing, there being no shortage of herring at the time:

IMPORTANT SALE OF SMOKE HOUSE EQUIPMENT
The smoke house, Island Wastrel (Late Mr. E.L. Veal)
1,100 mackerel cases. All bound with hoop iron.
2,500 herring barrels.
1 gas carbide lighting plant.

50 large fish baskets.
2 large washing baskets.
15 barrels of salt.
Quantity of sawdust chips.
5,000 bloater sticks.
6,000 kippering sticks.
5,000 kipper boxes.
500 half kipper boxes.
150 bundles tops, sides and bottoms kipper box wood.
15 bundles wooden hoops.

Nets

At the close of every fishing season where drift nets had been used, there was the task of mending the holes and broken meshes which had been caused by a multitude of reasons. The women folk had, for generations, been repairing nets in the lofts or in their homes, either as a profession or as the penalty of being in a fisherman's family. Our house was the same as many others, by the time the pilchard nets were finished the herring nets would be waiting their turn. Many fishermen had their own nets which they added to the nets already owned by the boat owner, so after their own nets were mended there were still the owner's nets to be repaired in the loft.

For those who intended to use their nets for crabbing, the winter months were spent in making nets in the home for the summer season. Being made from cotton there was no smell as there had been with the bark or pickled twine. The person making the net had a string belt with a hook around the waist, the first mesh was measured with a piece of wood called a "Mace-ster" and all other meshes were made the same size, unlike the camouflage nets made during the war, when every mesh was knotted on the mace-ster. Regardless of the type of net the needles had to be filled, and this was a task which fell to the boys.

Oilskin frocks, barwells and soggets

Every house Downlong had all three. If there were no men, there would probably be a woman engaged in the handling of fish or the making of the garments. The oil-skin frock has not changed in design over the years, only in its material. It is a frock without any buttons to catch in the mesh of the nets. A barwell is an apron with a rope loop around the top and two lanyards to tie around the middle. These were made from unbleached cotton and given two coats of linseed oil and hung out to dry on a wooden pole before other coats were applied. After being used they were given another coat at the end of the season. Sticking was one of their troubles and often flat paint was used to try to cure it. Soggets were aprons made of hessian, worn by men handling fish in cellars etc. Women often wore them over wrap-over aprons when counting herrings on the harbour front.

Children were often sent to the Fishermen's Co-op for a pint of oilskin oil, in a bottle kept for this purpose. The oil was applied with a piece of cloth.

Fish for friends

When fish were being landed the fishermen were never short of friends. During the herring season the other half of the town who had no direct contact with the fishing industry would soon be down to the harbour for a "feed of fish", often checking to see if the herring were hard roes (peas) or soft roes (milts) before departing with all fingers full of good size herring. No-one showed any concern for this stealing as "caabing" had been an accepted thing in the fishing industry that would not have been tolerated in any other industry. It should be mentioned that the fish which found so many good homes were the fishermens' and not the buyers'.

Men engaged in long-lining or trawling, always carried home a few fish for home consumption. It was often the boys' job to take around a ray, a whiting, a lagatta or perhaps "pea" of a ling or cod to sick or infirm friends, usually retired fishermen who could not get down to the boats. Those able to get to the harbour would stand on the sand near the punt, until a ray or a ling was thrown to them, then without a word from anyone they would depart for home.

The harbour at peace, most probably a Sunday as the pleasure boats are on their moorings and the shop doors are all closed. *c1935.*

The gas lanterns removed shows that it is summer at Back Roads, *c1900.* During nights of full moon in the winter the lights were left unlit.

The first improvements at Porthgwidden beach as the promenade leads to the steps to the Island. Washing and nets drying on the Island with a tent pitched on the front slope. The cars are parked on the area known as the Island Meadow, or sometimes the Cornfield. This was football and cricket pitch to countless boys and the staff of Cryséde factory. *c1947.*

A rare picture of sailing, motor and steam propulsion offloading cargoes of coal at Smeaton's Pier for the Gas Works and local coal merchants. *c1936.*

Cryséde silk works chimney smokes, the harbour junk awaits something bigger than the sailing vessel and fishermen load their wire crab pots on to their boats by the quay.

The steam coaster *Ben Gee* secured by the harbour junk, offloading coal at Smeaton's Pier. *1927.*

The railway station in the 1930's, complete with goods shed, crane, water tower, engine shed, waiting room, toilets and all that was required to despatch millions of fish in the winter and handle thousands of people in the summer.

BATHING AT PORTHMEOR BEACH, ST-IVES

G 13

Washing dries in Barnoon field, the site of the present Meadow flats. The studio of Mr. Lynn Pitt overlooks the beach opposite. 'Sunset' the only house on the seaward side, was built in 1927 with much controversy. Beach Road has only two houses. The track on the sand was probably made by the cart of Mr. W. Thomas as he hauled sand from the beach to build the Council houses at Ayr.

Dobles Wall, the centre of assembly before its alteration in more recent years. On the Plat by the Shore Shelter Lodge stands the boxed-in lifeboat winch. Below the people on the slipway timber is the hinged cover of the stormwater overflow. *1920's.*

An old picture of the Promenade before the railings and the fish plots which became the pavements. Mr. T. Thomas's boatbuilding workshop is next to the stone walls which were left after the Market Strand fire of 1915. *c1928.*

French fishermen with their colourful patches check their baskets of supplies which would be mainly bread, bartered for crabs. On occasions they would gather mussels from the rocks at the back of the Island and fill their water casks from the stream at Porthminster. *c1936.*

The highlight of the St. Ives Regatta was the race of the French crabbers. Although a sailing race there was often a little help from the engine.

The small fry were usually the first to catch the herring in St. Ives Bay. The *May* comes into this category, and it would seem that she has caught as many as she can carry. As they are still enmeshed it would probably be a morning shoot. Those hoping for a 'feed of fish' are alongside, and members of the family are at the bottom corner with a gurry of fish, probably waiting for it to be carried to the Wharf to be counted.

Before hygiene became popular, trawl fish spread on the ground for auction by the row or by the lot. The St. Ives Sea Scouts whaler and gig are the dark boats on the sand. *1938.*

WE December 19th 1908 *A warning to caabers.*

Letter from Mayor (part)

I have received a number of complaints lately to the effect that a large number of herrings are being stolen from the fishermen and the fishbuyers on the beach, especially in the evenings. It seems the inducement to the lads to steal the fish is that they can get people to purchase them.

I know fishermen are generous with their fish when they have a good catch, but with fish so scarce and dear as they are at present it is a great shame their generosity should be abused to the extent it is, in some cases by big lads.

I myself saw, on Wednesday evening, a lad offer 14 herring for one penny, the wholesale price of which was sevenpence.

John Pearce, Mayor

Weather wise

For those who earned their livings on the sea the weather was always a topic of conversation and concern. There being no BBC weather forecast all signs were carefully watched and respected.

Almost every home had a "bottle" which was a jar of coloured water and a bulbous bottle, its neck inserted into the liquid which rose or fell in the neck with the barometric pressure. Bottles were consulted, and influenced any decisions made.

The barometer, referred to as "the glass", in a box in the doorway of the lighthouse on Smeaton's pier, was the supreme authority over all fishing ventures. As boys we often had a look at it, but must confess we never understood it. The fact that the glass was stolen some years ago confirmed its worth. This was probably the Public Barometer provided by the Board of Trade in 1859.

Signs such as a ring around the moon, or sun dogs, were usually regarded as poor omens. There were also private signs seen by men not too keen to put to sea.

The weather during the winter herring season with a tidal harbour, was of life or death significance. The wind seemed always to be "drawing" i.e. coming from the west to a northerly direction. This would make the bay a bad place to be in, especially with no water in the harbour, which was the only refuge, or it would be "backing like fire" which meant a southerly wind and often rain. What fire had to do with it is not clear. The sign for exceptionally bad weather was when the glass was two tenths below twenty nine. At this mark all fishing was forgotten by the greater part of the fleet. The arrival of an easterly wind emptied the bay of herring that same night and although nets were shot in hope, catches would be very light.

The Pilots

One of the sights which has now disappeared from the bay was the transfer of the Trinity Pilot to and from coasters, either going to or coming from Hayle, Portreath or St. Ives harbour. The Pilot boat was the *Ada,* or a rowing skiff, the Pilot usually changing over in the Roads. After bringing one ship out he would often take a loaded ship in. On occasions of very poor weather it has been known for the Pilot to be unable to leave the ship and to be taken on to the ship's destination.

During the 1930's Dutch motor coasters were taking the trade from the British steam coaster, but both types with the odd sailing vessel were common sights, and with strong southerly gales there could be up to 50 ships of all types sheltering in the bay.

The Western Morning News used to publish the names of any ships "Sheltering St. Ives Bay". With ships in the bay boys used to go to the Library the next day to check on their names, but many were recognised as regulars, or their names were supplied by the Coastguard lookout.

Pilots have worked from St. Ives for many years. During 1870 they took 543 ships to Hayle, 107 to St. Ives and 91 to Portreath, a total of 741, for which the payment was £438. This was in the days of sail when a steam ship was used to tow them up the Hayle river.

Fishermens' Lodges

For most fishermen the Lodge was regarded as their second home. In fact some wives would say that their men spent more time there than at home. The Lodges rejoiced under such grand names as The Shamrock, The Rose, The Shore Shelter, The Bay View and The One and All. The first three still supply a need to the fishing fraternity. The One and All was the first to go. This stood on the sand at the bottom of Bethesda Hill. It had been undermined by the sea and collapsed into the water in November 1931. The Bay View, situated at the top of the breakwater behind Smeaton's pier, ended its days as a clubhouse. Being in a very exposed position it collapsed through stress of weather in the late 1970's.

The Lodges were "men only" preserves. Women rarely came in and children were just tolerated. In the centre was a coal fire, with lockers around the side containing the coal and firewood, and this has not changed over the years.

Most fishermen smoked a pipe and also chewed black roll tobacco. The floor was therefore covered with sand to absorb the surplus tobacco from the chewers and the jets which didn't quite make the stove. The sand was replaced every Saturday with clean milky sand, often from Porthmeor, as the harbour sand was not of the quality that it is today. The floor and lockers were scrubbed at the same time, often by men who, it is alleged, would never use a scrubber at home. The sanding of the floors continued until the 1960's by which time most of the chewers had passed on and canvas and carpet took its place.

Games of dominoes, cards, chequers or draughts, as well as rings, were played, but it was a meeting place where good shots were remembered and slight shots were best forgotten. Outside the Lodges was a space or plat for walking up and down. This would be the pre-arranged meeting place for crews to assemble to plan for the day's or night's fishing. Groups of men walking up and down were a source of amusement to the early visitors. Fishermen would leave home leaving the information that they could be found at "Hart's shop". This blacksmith's shop had been at one time on the site of the Primitive Methodist chapel, but had been moved towards the sea on rollers in 1830 for the chapel to be built. Its name has long outlived the building as a meeting place, but was generally accepted as being outside the present Shore Shelter.

The flag flying at half-mast marked the death of a member of the fishing community, in addition to the funeral card nailed on to the outside of the Lodge.

Flags of all nations, similar to a ship dressed overall, celebrated a wedding. Except for the use of glass cases instead of nails to display the cards all these customs are still observed.

The Shamrock Lodge was formally opened on 12th October 1901 on its present site by Councillor W.Faull. The Shore Shelter was opened the same day, but this was on the sand, not in its present position. The Rose Lodge was also situated on the sand near the entrance to Court Cocking. This was opened on 19th October 1901 by Mr. E.H.Best, when speeches were made by Messrs. W.Herbert, J.Hollow, W.Badcock and L.M.Grier, to celebrate the fact that all expenses had been cleared.

The One and All commenced life in June 1904 on the harbour sand which at that time was safe from the sea. Boats were built alongside and fairs held nearby, but changes in other parts of the harbour no doubt contributed to the sea returning to its high water mark, and in so doing undermined the building in the mid-1930's.

Alterations and extension to the promenade made it necessary to move the Shore and the Rose to more substantial positions, so in 1918 a bequest of £300 from Sir Edward Hain paid for the present Lodges on the plat, where they now stand. At the time of building they were flanking a gentlemen's public convenience. This has since been changed to a public shelter, which owing to vandalism has now been closed. St. Ives Town Council still own the land on which the Lodges were built, and a ground rent of five pence a year is paid. The Shamrock has been protected from the sea by a wall built in 1940 to prevent Hitler landing his troops and tanks. No doubt it saved the Lodge from damage on many occasions and helps to give it some privacy.

6 WRECK AND RESCUE

The lifeboat

The launching of the lifeboat, whether for service or practice, was always the star attraction for the children of Downlong. The arrival of the first motor lifeboat in 1933 ended a 30-odd year association with a pulling and sailing boat with the local sounding name of *James Stevens No.10*. At this time every fishing boat in the harbour had been driven by an engine, so it was just as well that the older men had been brought up in sail. Within weeks the old boat was back again as a pleasure boat, renamed *Patricia Mary*. She was running trips from Porthminster beach, but with the addition of an engine.

With six blue oars on the starboard side and six white oars to port, the 12-oared *James Stevens* had a crew of 15 men. It was the rule that those who went on a service launch would have a trip on the next practice. For a service launch the Cox'n would put six life-jackets into the boat for his selected men, the rest of the crew being made up by the first on the scene. The main thing for the launchers was to get hold of a badge. This arm-band was thrown from the top window of the boathouse and entitled the man, on its return to the boathouse, to a payment of 5/- for a summer launch and 7/6 in winter, but no doubt this fee had been different at other periods of history. This money was hard earned when the tide was out, those pulling the ropes having to wade into the sea up to their armpits before the boat floated from her carriage. A winter immersion was a chilling experience as well as a soaking for their clothing, possibly their Sunday best. Not everyone had payment for this task, but with little money about every shilling was most welcome. The launching was always accompanied by much whistle blowing and shouts of "Hunchie-baw-ee". At least that is what it sounded like, and it seemed to have the desired effect.

A motor lifeboat being heavier than a rowing boat, and so many men being away at war, a motor tractor was first used for a service launch on the 12th February 1940, so scores of men were made redundant overnight.

Fifty years ago everyone Downlong turned out at night for a launch, either to help or enquire the reason for the maroon. Now it is only a handful of launchers, and even less spectators. This is partly due to the number of Downlong residents with no maritime connections.

The history of the St. Ives lifeboat has been well covered in other publications, so a mention of the boathouse will not be out of place. The first known boathouse is the nearest building to the Island gate. From this house the boat was launched at Porthmeor or Porthgwidden, according to weather conditions, and was built by Messrs. Cothey and Thomas Burrell for £142 in 1860.

In 1867 a boathouse was built on the present site, there being no West pier or promenade, and the boat came straight out on to the sand. A small slipway was built in 1890, possibly because of the movement of sand caused by the building of the Victorian extension to Smeaton's pier. The building was formerly known as the Old Custom House and rebuilt by Mr. Sampson Noall for £140.

The building of the West Pier in 1894 made it necessary to build a larger slipway in 1899. This was almost completely covered by the extension of the promenade in 1922. Since then the boat has been pulled across the harbour front to the widened Chy an Chy slipway.

In January 1899 the St. Ives boat went to Hayle Bar to render assistance to a steamer which was aground. Having had three men washed overboard and no acceptance of her help, the boat entered Hayle. At evening the authorities at St. Ives decided to send horses with the carriage to Hayle to get the boat back on station. It was then found that owing to the building work it was not possible to get the carriage up over the hill to the Market House without removing the wheels and pulling the carriage and wheels up the steep incline with block and tackle. On the return from Hayle with the boat the reverse procedure had to be followed. The writer of the account expressed concern lest valuable time should be lost if the boat was required at Carbis Bay or Lelant.

On the 1st January 1900 a new and larger lifeboat for the St. Ives station arrived by rail at Hayle, named the *James Stevens No.10.* She was brought to St. Ives by water on the following day and the old lifeboat *Exeter* was placed on the West pier under coverings pending her removal to the Institution's depot at Poplar.

On the night of 6th November 1900 the *James Stevens* was launched on her first service when a number of herring boats were caught in the bay in a N.N.W. gale anchoring with the other boats in the Roads. She accompanied them into harbour. The gig *Fortitude* was afterwards found bottom up on Carrack Gladden beach and three of her crew of four were drowned. On the morning of the 7th November the *Exeter* was again used to take the crew from the ketch *Star of Scilly* before she was smashed on to the rocks at Porthminster Point, this being her last service. On the same afternoon the *James Stevens* put to sea to escort the ketch *Foundling* being towed by the lugger *Ripple* into the harbour, after having shown signals of distress six miles north of St. Ives Head. After 15 months on the West pier, on the 21st March 1901, the *Exeter* was taken to the railway station and sent to Poplar, London, where she was subsequently broken up.

On Christmas night in 1923 the launching of the lifeboat to the aid of the fishing boat *Peggy* which was showing a "flambeau" near Godrevy, was not without incident, when the boat was held up on the slipway for six minutes. This resulted in a letter in the local press from Cox'n. Wedge, complaining of *"undue interference on the part of over zealous or irresponsible persons taking charge, instead of acting under the Launching Authority"* The fact that it was Christmas night probably had much to do with it.

Until the arrival of the tractor, the carriage had always been steered by two pairs of shafts which had been designed for horses, and Messrs. R. and N.Phillips, who were head launchers, were men who used horses every day in their work as carriers at the railway station, but the last time that horses were used at St. Ives is uncertain.

Wrecks and losses

The occasion of shipwreck and loss figures high in boyhood memory, and in six years we had our share.

On the afternoon of 12th September 1934 news was received in the town of the loss of the fishing boat *Amelia,* which had been run down by a French steamer *Mousse le Moyec* in dense fog while crabbing to the westward of St. Ives. I can remember it being explained to me that the two sons of Mr. Stevens across the road would not be coming back, and Mr. Penberthy of the next house up the road from Mr. Stevens would also not be returning.

At times of distress at sea the men used to gather on the Island by the seat at the corner of the factory, now St. Nicholas Court flats, and that day they seemed to be willing the *Amelia* to come into view around Clodgy Point before accepting the inevitable and leaving for home. I have always remembered that day. The *Mousse le Moyec* on passage from Plymouth to Cardiff in ballast, broke down and drifted ashore on rocks near Hartland Point on the 6th December 1940.

On the morning of Saturday 25th January 1935 the Bideford ketch *Cicelia* which had been moored against Smeaton's pier, broke her ropes while her crew were on the pier. She drove across the harbour entrance and grounded on Pednolver rocks. That happened at 8.30am, too early to be seen by most boys, but she wasn't broken to pieces immediately, so became an attraction. The following Monday the spars and engine were sold for £30 at public auction, and the ship broke up on the rocks. This ship had been built in Jersey in 1867 and was the last Channel Island vessel engaged on the Newfoundland cod trade when sold in 1914.

In June 1936 the Hull ketch *St. Austell* showed signals of distress when in a leaking condition six miles off the Head. The lifeboat *Caroline Parsons* towed her into the harbour where she remained for several weeks. On each high tide she filled with water and the boys' favourite sport was to man the pumps and help pump her out. This boat had become a regular casualty at St. Ives. On three occasions she had been in trouble off St. Ives Head, each time with a different crew, but always from Swansea to Guernsey with coal. On discharging her cargo at St. Ives and some repairs she sailed in late July for Plymouth. A strong south west wind sprang up after her departure and anxiety was felt for her safety.

November 2nd 1936 brought the most profitable wreck

to the vicinity of St. Ives, with no loss of life, the cargo being warmly received by one and all. The 5685 ton *Bessemer City* with general cargo from California, after dropping off 300 tons of raisins at Liverpool, was on passage to London in heavy mist and rain and ran aground on rocks near Pen Enys point, Trevalgan cliffs being a more familiar name for the locality. The *Caroline Parsons,* launched around midnight, brought back 10 of the crew on her first trip. Her second brought back 17 men and after refuelling she brought back the six remaining officers. With the ship breaking in two within a few hours and later into three, the cargo was released and with the flowing tides crates of tinned fruit and salmon littered the shore line as far as Newquay. It being the start of the herring season there were plenty of boats available to clear the water of cases which might well have been a hazard to other shipping. With the labels being washed from the tins there was always the chance that a tin of pears might turn out to be peaches for Sunday tea. Although not everybody had cases most people had a few tins during this bonanza period. Large blocks of sultanas also came ashore, but the fuel oil had fouled them and rendered them useless.

July 1937 brought another shipwreck with the grounding of the *Aida Lauro* of Naples. On passage from Liverpool to Hull with a cargo of cotton seed, linseed, peanuts and cement, she struck rocks between Pendeen and St. Just. Fifteen crew members were brought to St. Ives by the *Caroline Parsons* and sixteen came ashore at Pendeen in her own boats. The wreck being so far west of the town and the cargo not suitable for salvage, not much interest was aroused in the town. With the tide being particularly low difficulty was experienced in floating the lifeboat, which grounded after launching from her carriage. The reports of the day state that the entire St. Ives Police Force; Sgt. Osborne, P.C.'s Jones, James, Appleton, Keast and Wilkinson, discarded their helmets and tunics to help float the boat using skids.

The loss of the *Alba* and the capsizing of the *Caroline Parsons* on Porthmeor beach on the night of 31st January 1938 has been well covered in other "Wreck" books. The loss of five men on our doorstep happened in front of hundreds of people who had gathered on the Island and Porthmeor cliff, expecting to see a straightforward rescue. If it wasn't for the townsfolk or if the wreck had been further from the town, there would have been few survivors that night. Great bravery was shown in entering the water and pulling men from the sea among the Island rocks. If the same situation arose again no doubt there would be a disaster of great magnitude, with few on shore to help.

The stripping of the lifeboat of engine and useful parts was followed by the burning on the Island rocks of the remains of the boat, but this was not before every boy managed to get a piece of the boat as a souvenir. Half model lifeboats were shaped by the model makers from wood of the boat, and brass nails from the ashes that remained were eagerly sought. At school the wreck was portrayed in crayon and paint at every art lesson. Salvage work on cargo and fittings went on all the summer of 1938 and buckets of coal were retrieved by boys and men at low water.

The loss of the *John and Sarah Eliza Stych* on the night of 23rd January 1939 has also been well covered in other publications. As boys around the harbour these were the men that we knew. Those who had given us cigarette cards or played rugby at the Recreation Ground. Suffice to say that part of Downlong died that night. The same has happened in other fishing communities and it takes time to recover. There were no drawing lessons at school, no souvenirs of the boat and much discussion in high places, with talk of breakwaters and larger boats, all of which came to nought with the outbreak of the second world war.

Strange as it may seem, the house across the road was again affected. This time Mr. Stevens was to lose his son-in-law, Mr. Matthew Barber, from that same house, and again on the 30th November 1954 with the sinking of the Hain steamer *Tresillian* off the Irish coast, he lost his grandson, who had lost his father in the *Amelia*. All of which bears out what I had mentioned in the early chapter "Paternal and Maternal" that most families had similar stories of loss at sea. Again, in 1980, Timothy Lander, a great grandson of the late Mr. Stevens, was drowned in an accident whilst fishing.

7 FAIRS, FESTIVALS & SPECIAL OCCASIONS

Fairs

In early years Fairs were held on the foreshore near the arches, but owing to changes in the harbour causing the tide to cover this area, and alterations at the foot of Dick's Hill, they were held on the Island Meadow from the early 1920's.

Steam traction engines towing trailers and caravans came through the town early in the morning. No damage was ever done to any property and one driver with only one hand was greatly admired for his driving. Many modern car drivers would be ashamed of their efforts to enter Island Road if they had known how these men negotiated the same corner with ease.

The Fairs were usually small, no big wheels, just roundabouts and swings and the usual amusements, but at the entrance there was always a stannen selling toffee apples where the owner made clidgey nicey which he mixed and stretched on a hook before cutting into lengths for sale.

At the end of their stay the Fair moved out early before anyone was astir and was on its way to Penzance or Redruth, to be followed in a day or so by local people who also patronised the bigger Fairs in these towns.

WE Sept 1933 HERE AND THERE by Wayfarer.

I saw part of Mr. Jones' Fair being hauled through up the street on Wednesday morning. If the Fair attracted more spectators on the Island than it did at the Market House and in Tregenna Place then Mr. Jones will soon be in St. Ives again. Mr. Jones deserves a word of praise. Every time he brings his Arcadian Joys to St. Ives he gives periods of gross takings to charities, and has more than once had a dance on the Dodgem floor. These are kindly actions and should surely bring a reward.

The Regatta

The regatta in the bay was of great interest, as everyone knew the men and boats involved. The *Mamie* was the biggest, with unlikely challengers like the *Gladys May,* the *Seagull* and the *Ivor.* The greatest interest was in the skiffs, the blue-painted *Bluebird* and the red-painted *Boy George* always enjoyed a big following and aroused much interest on the Friday night before the race, when racing masts were fitted.

The French crabbers working from the bay often entered as well. This was the race that the boys enjoyed. Not having seen the sailing of our own fleet, we were pleased to see the last of the Bretons that were still using sail as their only means of propulsion.

WE August 1929 Motor gig race for 12 hp Kelvin engines.

1. Daisy (J.Cothey)   2. James Francis (W.Care)   3. Active (J.P.Veal)

WE 1933 The strong SW wind compelled the cancellation of all the races with the exception of the yacht race.

1. Mamie (R.Paynter) 2. Seagull (E.C.Paynter) 3. Gladys May (E.C.Paynter)

Three French crabbers put into the bay for shelter and, on being approached, their skippers willingly consented to sail.

1. Pic-Vert   2. Albert Robers   3. La Bousse Mor (All of Camaret)

WE May 1934 HERE AND THERE by Wayfarer.
SKIFFS

Thursday afternoon had its significance in St. Ives harbour for the Bluebird, Mr. H.C.Comley's new skiff, had her trial trip. The crew comprised of Mr. G.Wedge (owner of Boy George) and his brother Mr. C.Wedge, Mr. T.Honey and Mr.Comley. The West pier and "Castle" were lined with enthusiasts discussing the setting of the sails and a hundred other details.

Hayle Regatta

It would be true to say that everyone went to Hayle Regatta. First of all there was the novelty of the train trip, there were the swimming events, the greasy pole, the flour and soot fight, and, of course, the sailing events, our own skiffs being taken over for the races.

The banks would be lined with people, with carts and stannens selling everything necessary to make it a great day. In the evening there was the carnival, and finally the train ride back home, altogether a very special day.

Frenchie Craboo

The arrival of the French crabbers in the bay was usually looked upon as a sign of bad weather to come. It was not unusual to see twenty or thirty boats on the horizon during the summer months. Most of the boats had a single mast, but some bigger boats had a mizzen as well. Many of these boats had no engines, or, if they did, they used them very sparingly. Their "batu" had a small engine and from this small but strongly built boat the crab pots were worked. It was therefore common practice to stay at the fishing ground rather than sail into the bay in the light summer breezes. It took severe weather or some sort of damage for the crabbers to come into the harbour. This was because the live shellfish were kept in the well of the boat. This compartment was slotted for the sea to flow through, and to stay in a tidal harbour with the sea out was not appreciated by the fish. At regular intervals the boats would sail to Newlyn to transfer their fish to a carrier to be taken to France.

Quite often the Frenchmen came ashore to get bread and water. Whilst ashore there was usually a visit to the Sloop Inn at the same time. A basket of crabs was often used for barter. Sometimes they landed on 'Mester beach to fill a barrel with water from the stream. Some men would go to the rocks at the back of the Island to fill a bag with mussels. The men were very clean. Their clothing was covered with patches, not always of the same colour as the original cloth. On their feet they wore wooden clogs and some had inner tubes from motor car tyres nailed to the clogs to make them into sea boots. They were never seen to post or receive any letters, and apart from their own countrymen had few contacts ashore. Boys used to speak to them with always the same question *"Plenty long-goose Johnnie?"* to which there was always the same reply *"No plenty"*. The boys were pleased to think they had spoken French, but would have been very confused if they had received any other answer.

Batus tied to the quay steps were only asking to be borrowed. These boats were heavy to scull and there was always some doubt as to the reaction of the returning fishermen. Very often if the men were coming down over the old quay it would be thought prudent to head for the new quay and make a quick exit. It was always feared that the Frenchmen would take boys aboard and back to France. This was of course without foundation as the men were never in trouble ashore. Afloat things were a little different. On occasions *HMS Dart,* the Fishery Protection vessel for this area, would be seen towing in a crabber which had been caught fishing inside the three mile limit. The gear was often confiscated and the Skipper fined as well. The gear was often stacked on the old quay until bought back and fishing would commence again.

Almost all the boats came from Camaret in Brittany. Many of the men had been boys when they arrived for the first time. Indeed in the early 1900's French boats used to moor behind the breakwater. In very early days Breton fishermen lived on the Island at a spot known to us boys as the cowshed. This was from when cows grazed there. They used 'Widden for their landing place. History has it that as a result of finding nets on the beach after the return of the Frenchmen, the St. Ives drift net fishery was started. The Frenchmen of my boyhood were excellent fishermen and fine sailors. Having missed the St. Ives sailing fleet we were in time to see how these men handled their boats, which made up for our loss.

***SWS 22 August 1908** A FRENCH INVASION. Between 120 and 130 French crabbers are sheltering in St. Ives Bay from a strong southerly wind. As each boat carries a crew of four hands about 500 Frenchmen are visiting our shores.*

Warships

For most boys the arrival of warships in the Bay was looked forward to from the time of the preliminary announcement. Often the ships were opened to the public and at night they were lit up and on occasions gave searchlight displays.

At a Council meeting in June 1928 the Mayor read a letter to the effect that *HMS Tiger* proposed visiting St. Ives from 14th to 16th July and would be open for inspection from 2.30pm to 5.30pm on the Sunday. Alderman Lawry thought this dangerous as it would inaugurate a new fashion in St. Ives, and moved that the ship be open on Saturday instead of Sunday. As a corporate body they should not give up anything that would desecrate the Sabbath. On the 7th July the visit of the ship was cancelled. The battle cruiser *Tiger* had been heavily engaged at Jutland in the first world war, but was scrapped before the second war began.

The town was decorated with flags and bunting in July 1930 to welcome for a four day visit the Fifth Destroyer Flotilla comprising *HM Ships Wallace, Walker, Watchman, Vimy, Vortigern* and *Warwick*, to be joined later by *Tetrarch* and *Sesame.*

Owing to a strong gale the two submarines *HMS Perseus* and *Proteus* sought shelter in the Bay in October 1930, as also did the German tug *Seefalke* usually found on her station in Mounts Bay.

In July 1933 the Royal Navy showed its strength in the Bay with the battleship *Valiant* and the first visit to the Bay of an aircraft carrier *HMS Furious* with the destroyers *Vega, Walker, Wallace* and *Champion.*

The visit of *HMS Foresight* in June 1937 was the last visit of any note. For three days she was open to the public and hundreds availed themselves of the opportunity.

The visit of the new cruiser *HMS Exeter* in July 1932 also brought the floodlighting of the war memorial gardens, with fairy lights in the trees, all arranged by the local Chamber of Commerce. There was some feeling caused by the Council not allowing boats to be used to transport visitors to the ship on the Sunday during the visit.

HMS Exeter came into the news in 1939 with her fight, together with *HMS Ajax* and *HMNZS Achilles,* against the German battleship *Graf Spee.* After repair from severe damage she went to the Pacific and was sunk by Japanese surface craft in the South Java Sea on the 1st March 1942. *HMS Valiant* spent the early years of the war in the Mediterranean and was damaged by a two-man Italian torpedo on the 19th December 1941 in harbour at Alexandria. *HMS Furious* survived the War and saw service in the North Atlantic and Arctic. On 16/17 March 1941 *HMS Walker* under the command of Captain D.G.MacIntyre, when leading seven warships of the Fifth Escort Group, sank *U99.* Kapitan Leutnant Otto Kretschmer, the Commander of *U99*, one of the leading U-boat aces, spent the rest of the War in Canada as a prisoner of war.

HMS Foresight was severely punished whilst defending the torpedoed cruiser *HMS Edinburgh* against attack by German destroyers in May 1942. After her return from the Arctic she went to the Mediterranean, was torpedoed by Italian aircraft and sank on 13th August 1942.

Of the ships in the 1930 visit, the *Walker* has already been mentioned; *Vortigern* was sunk by an E-boat off Cromer on the 15th March 1942; *Warwick* was torpedoed and sunk by *U413* off the North Cornish coast on the 20th February 1944; *Watchman* sank *U 1195* in the English Channel in 1945 and *H.M.Submarine Perseus* was lost in the Mediterranean when torpedoed by the Italian submarine *Enrico Toti* on 1st January 1941. The *Proteus* was in

Chinese waters on the outbreak of war, and went to the Mediterranean until 1943, when she was used for training in U.K. waters until scrapped in 1946.

Show Days

Once a year the artists of the town opened their studios to the general public. Show Day was quite an event with visitors trying to find the studios which were often hidden in so many of the out of the way places. With the decline in fishing net lofts were being turned into studios often with only an old sail dividing one artist from another.

Very few Downlong people bothered to avail themselves of this free show, but an excellent relationship existed with the artists, except when one was unwise enough to set up an easel on a Sunday. A "flink" of a doormat, or even a stream of water meandering down between the legs of the easel would make the artist understand that he had chosen the wrong day to paint. At this time there were probably forty to fifty traditional artists painting in St. Ives and the Show Day was their way of showing their work, especially the pictures which had been selected for the Royal Academy. These were later loaded into a special railway container parked in Back Roads.

One of the artists who opened his house to the public was my neighbour Alfred Wallis. So much has been written about him by people who never knew him that it is a pity that this harmless old man had so little reward for his work except the pleasure he experienced in giving his paintings away, often with the reward of some well squeezed tubes of oil paint. Surely he would have chuckled to hear himself described as a primitive genius in his old age, and to have a plaque fixed to his outside wall far exceeds any other traditional local artist. In 1941 he was taken to Madron Workhouse, but before going he had left with my Grandmother sufficient funds for his burial at Barnoon. On his death in August 1942 plans were made for a collection among the artists to avoid a pauper's funeral, but the Undertaker was then advised of the money held for that purpose, and after being laid to rest, the grave was covered with tiles suitably decorated by Mr. Bernard Leach, and is probably the most valuable gravestone in Barnoon cemetery.

Capt. Borlase Smart was much involved with the Sea Scout movement. He, together with John Park and John Barclay, were well-known and appreciated Downlong, even if, when they were painting harbour scenes, their boats didn't always look exactly like the originals.

The idea of Show Days for artists ceased to exist with the opening of new galleries in the town since the Second World War, which is kinder than saying that many of the pictures are beyond the understanding of ordinary mortals.

SWS In June 1889 we are informed that the St. Ives painters are returning to their studios, fresh from the Royal Academy and other well known exhibitions. Among those already at work are Mr. and Mrs. Adrian Stokes, Mr.and Mrs. Harewood Robinson, Mr. and Mrs. E.E.Simmons, Messrs. W.Eadie, Louis Grier, W.H.Titcombe, E.W.Blomefield and Julius Olsson.

WE May 1923 "Round the Town" by Observer.

The artists have readily acceded to the request of the Rev. Rutter to alter the date of the Show Day so that it would not clash with the opening of the new Primitive Methodist Sunday School.

WE On Show Day in 1927 there were no fewer than 35 exhibitors, and although the number is rather less than usual it was generally agreed that the works on view marked a distinctive advance on recent years.

WE In 1929, 14 St. Ives painters had pictures exhibited at the Royal Academy in London.

Feast Monday - silver ball

The question of whether the silver ball should be a game between two teams or a fiasco where the big boys monopolise the ball until the time of its return, has always been a hot potato at St. Ives. It also had periods of revival and decline. For the most part I can only remember it being a "non-event" as far as most of the boys were concerned. By the time we became the big boys we were working on the day of the Feast as we left school at fourteen years of age.

SWS 1890 Extracts from Robert Hunt's 'Popular Romances of the West of England' show that a pole is erected on the beach and each side strives to get *"the oftenest to the goold i.e. the pole. The other side manfully strove to keep them out and send their opponents as great a distance from the pole as possible"*. Whether there were one or two "goolds" is not clear, or how many were in each team.

In 1919, after a lapse of five years caused by the Great War, a rugby match; St. Ives versus RAF Mullion, was played but there was no mention of the silver ball that year.

The St. Ives Feast of 1920 caused more confusion, the precise date of the Feast giving rise to a difference of opinion. Most of the social functions were arranged for one Sunday and Monday, but the Vicar announced that the Dedication Festival of the Parish Church would take place the following Sunday. The old custom of hurling the silver ball was revived, and the proceedings followed with interest.

In 1921 we find that the old custom of hurling the silver ball was revived, the ball being thrown up on the Malakoff, the second revival in two years, but it must have been below par as for 1922 we have two teams mentioned and the word 'revival' again.

WE 1921 The Old Cornwall Society recently offered the town a silver ball, that by it the good old custom may be kept up and the youths of the town always play at hurling on Feast Day.

At a game reported in the Echo, in the first half T.Andrews scored for the Whites. In the second half J.W.Cocking and H.Corin got two goals for the Plains. Where this game was played is not clear, but Porthminster beach was the venue for 1923, when two capital sides were selected with Mr.C.P.Bennetts, captain of the Reds, and his son Mr.P.Bennetts in charge of the Whites. B.T.Veal goaled for the Reds (2) and Paul Trevorrow for the Whites.

The 1930 occasion was a shambles. As the ball was being run across the Wharf it was hurled into the harbour and no further play could be indulged in until the tide receded.

It seems that some lessons had been learned in time for the 1932 Feast. The Echo reported that two teams representing Uplong and Downlong were to play on Monday morning, money prizes to be given to both teams. The teams selected were:

Downlong - R.Cocking, J.N.Stevens, W.Noall, J.Wedge, R.Uren, C.Noall, J.Polmeor, R.Nichols, J.Bassett, E.Murt, H.Beard, R.J.Uren.

Uplong - W.Baker, W.Phillips, Jos.Tanner, J.& B.Witheridge,B.Gay, S.Stoneman, A.Stratton, F.C.Blewett, J.Woolcock, I.Curnow, R.Curnow.

A large crowd assembled in the precincts of the harbour to witness the ancient game of hurling. The ball was thrown by the Mayor (Mr. W.R.Hollow) then the teams of twelve representatives of Uplong and Downlong wrestled with each other for half an hour. R.Nichols scored for Downlong, but at the breather the scores were level, G.Paynter having scored a long range goal. Eventually Jackie Woolcock not only secured the lead but completed the hat-trick. Result: Uplong 4 goals, Downlong 1 goal. The Mayor presented 2s.6d. each to the members of the winning team and 1s.0d. to the losers.

May Day

Only a few children rose early to welcome this special day. The sound of May horns was heard in some parts of the town and "Peeweeps" made from the bark of the sycamore tree helped swell the noise. Spring flowers tied to a piece of wood and bunches of flowers were taken to school and the maypole was danced around in the playground, but this was as far as the celebrations went.

SWS In the 1880's May Day was known in St. Ives as Cream Day. Large numbers of boys and girls went "A-Maying" in the early morning and returned with large bunches of flowers, both wild and cultivated. The schools gave a half-day holiday, which the youngsters used to parade the streets with tin trumpets, much to the annoyance of the townsfolk. Described as "a most hideous and unmusical sound" the noise of their trumpets woke many from refreshing sleep.

WE At the 1922 meeting of the St. Ives Old Cornwall Society, particular interest was shown in an old custom of going up to Ayr on May morning for a treat of sour milk cut into dice and sold from a wooden washing tray, to be eaten with sugar or with "thunder and lightning" (bread and cream with zig-zags of treacle), this being connected with the old custom of claiming cream in payment for an open fern or a May bough. It was observed, with regret, that maypoles and "Kings of May" which once figured in borough accounts, were no longer seen, and St. Ives contributed scarcely one toot of a May horn.

WE The May Day of 1925 was recorded as having passed very quietly at St. Ives, there being little to distinguish it from any other day of the month.

Sunday School Treats

The 1930's were about ten years too late with regard to Band of Hope or Tea Treat marches. Something which had been one of the major events of the year had now become very much a mothers' and childrens' tea. The men were not involved in such numbers. Prior to the first world war all the treats were held before the men sailed for the North Sea fisheries.

At Zion we often went by train to Payne's Picnic Grounds at Carbis Bay. Although a very short ride it was a novelty. Races were run and a saffron bun as big as a tea plate was eaten. Bun tickets for extra buns were fourpence each. There was a cast iron hen which laid an egg for a penny, and rowing boats on the lake. This site is now the

Cottage Hotel. At other times we went to the Tea Gardens at Hawke's Point, just beside the railway crossing. We also went by motor coach to Praa Sands, Sennen or Gwithian towans. Then for a change we would go to Man's Head, Carthew. This meant a lot of work for the few men involved, as besides the trestles, tables and crockery, the iron boiler had to be carried, also the wood, coal and water.

SWS July 1889 *Lady Huntingdon's Sunday School had their annual treat*
on Thursday at Payne's Picnic Ground, Carbis Bay.

SWS July 1890 *St. Ives Bible Christian Sunday School had their annual Treat on Thursday. The School's new banner headed the procession to a field at Trenwith. The Salvation Army had their annual outing to Hawke's Point on Tuesday.*

SWS August 1890 *St. Ives Wesley and New Connexion Sunday Schools had their annual outing on Thursday at Mr. Payne's and Mrs. Williams, Carbis Bay. About 500 children and 200 adults went by rail in addition to a large number who strolled along the cliffs.*

SWS *CARBIS BAY PICNIC GROUND*
(Close to the Railway Station)

J.W.Payne & Son beg to inform their patrons and the public generally that their new grounds, situated on a beautiful slope overlooking the sands and beach and laid out in terraces, seats, shrubs and grass squares, with a number of Tea Houses and various amusements including swings, hobby horses, skittles, alpine railway, are now open.

Every convenience for large or small parties.

Sunday School and Band of Hope children supplied with cups and hot water on the grass at 1d. each. Adults provided (in the house) with earthenware and hot water at 2d. each.

WE June 1919 *Zion School Treat at Carthew led by the Salvation Army band. It is unfortunate the local schools do not fall into line with the Education Authority in refer-*

116

ence to annual Tea Treats. The Council and National schools in St. Ives close for the whole week for Treats, and in spite of this one of the schools had their annual Treat on Thursday last which necessitated the school closing on that afternoon.

WE July 1921 *St. Peters Street U.M.Sunday School scholars paraded the lower part of the town and adjourned to the Public Hall owing to the wet weather. Zion School Treat, owing to wet weather, might have resulted in heavy financial loss, had not members of the church, with other friends, bought the surplus provisions, whereby the loss only amounted to a few shillings.*

WE August 1921 *Primitive Methodists School Treat. The weather was kind enough on Thursday to permit the teachers and scholars to parade the town. All at home turned out, but the absence of the men at Newlyn on the pilchard fishery was noticeable.*

WE July 1924 *St. Peters Street U.M.C. School Treat. The annual School Treat assembled in the schoolroom, headed by the St. Ives Prize Band, marched to the War Memorial, where a beautiful wreath was laid by Superintendents M.Stevens and W.Knight, then proceeded to Carthew.*

Band of Hope

The Band of Hope Gala was the annual parade of the Teetotal Society which had been formed in St. Ives in 1838. Those taking part in earlier days had worn their aprons and coloured sashes of office and were addressed by a speaker on the merits of abstention from drink.

The Sunday Schools of the town partook in these processions which in most cases seemed to be quite a long march for young children. Little wonder that it was held before the men departed on the North Sea fishery.

SWS June 1890 *After a harbour demonstration three bands accompanied the large procession around the town. About 1,000 little ones partook of tea in a field at Wheal Margery and nearly 3300 adults sat down to tea.*

WE June 1919 *After a lapse of four years St.Ives United*

Band of Hope Festival was held on Tuesday last at Carthew in fine weather. There was a large procession in the afternoon, led by St. Ives Silver Band. After perambulating the principal streets of the town the children repaired to Carthew where they were served with buns and tea. A public tea followed, to which a good number sat down.

WE 1921 A meeting of representatives of various Sunday Schools agreed that scholars of each School combine in a demonstration on Midsummer day. The order of procession was decided by ballot; Wesleyan, St. Peter's Street, Primitive, Salvation Army, Congregational, Bedford Road. It is hoped a field will be secured for the unique event, as this is the first time that the Schools have combined with the Band of Hope.

WE 1921 Midsummer Gala. The teachers and scholars assembled on the Island and the procession accompanied by the St. Ives Town and Salvation Army bands marched through the streets to Trenwith Park. It was one of the longest processions ever seen at St. Ives, over 3,000 tea tickets were disposed of.

WE June 1922 Band of Hope Gala. All the non-conformist Sunday Schools of the town met at the Island. After forming a huge procession they paraded the town and repaired to a field at Trenwith.

WE June 1925. Band of Hope Gala was held at the new Recreation Ground. As usual the children and teachers of the various Sunday Schools paraded the town, carrying flags and banners, accompanied by the St. Ives Town and Salvation Army bands..

WE July 1931 Band of Hope Gala (spoiled by rain at Midsummer). It has been decided to give the children a free tea (buns), and sports, at the Recreation Ground on Bank Holiday 3rd August. The children will meet at the Island at 1.30pm, sing the hymn "Tell me the old, old story" and proceed to the Ground led by the St. Ives Town and Salvation Army Bands. J.R.Cothey, Treasurer. E.P.Curnow, Secretary.

WE June 1936 St. Ives Band of Hope. At a meeting of representatives of each of the Methodist, Zion and Salvation Army Sunday Schools, it was decided to hold the Band of Hope Gala on Thursday at Lodge Lane Field in the grounds of Tregenna Castle Hotel. It will be noticed that the St. Ives Silver Prize band has not been engaged, and the Committee wishes to point out that this is because the funds will no longer stand this expense.

What was probably the last Band of Hope held in St. Ives was advertised in the Western Echo in June 1939:

St. Ives Band of Hope
Annual Gala at Carthew
on Thursday 22nd June
Children will congregate on the Island at 2.30pm
After singing a hymn, a procession will be formed to perambulate the town. Teas served at Carthew from 4.30pm.

Armistice Day

The sound of the lifeboat maroon marked the commencement of the two minutes silence at 11 o'clock on the 11th November. Except for the cry of the gulls over the harbour everything stopped moving in the town as carts and lorries stopped in their tracks.

At school the poppy sellers had already been around. It was expected for everyone to have a poppy. A penny was all that was required for an ordinary poppy. The teachers had a poppy with a leaf, which cost sixpence. None of those lost during the war had been known to the scholars, so there was no reading of the names of the fallen. The war had been over for fifteen years and more, therefore the ceremony had been diminished from former years as far as the school was concerned, but there were many wreaths laid at the town War Memorial.

The following report in the Western Echo of the 1928 Armistice Day at the school is worth recording:-

Over 700 children at St. Ives Council School celebrated the Armistice Day anniversary in a manner which will indelibly stamp upon their young minds the true meaning of the 11th day of the 11th month.

In the Boys' School the proceedings started at 10.50 by the singing of 'Lest we forget', followed by the reading by Mr.W.Lawry M.B.E. of the names of 83 Old Boys who made the supreme sacrifice. Twelve of the senior boys and twelve senior girls later marched to the War Memorial and reverently placed a wreath on behalf of the boys and girls of St. Ives Schools.

Allan Apple Day

Halloween had only one meaning for St. Ives children. There were no witches or broomsticks, no tricks or treats. It was the one night when children were eager to go to bed early, and also keen to get out the following morning, for underneath their pillow would be the largest apple it was possible to buy. October 31st might be All Saints Day to the Church, but to us it was Allan Apple Day, when all children ate the apple that had been such a temptation the previous night. The type of apple did not matter, the main thing was that it had to be large, and the fruit shops got in a good supply to meet the demand.

Fair Mo

The one Saturday in the year that was something special was Fair Mo. All the pocket money for many weeks had also been given with the advice 'save it for Fair Mo'. When it came it was like a damp squib. Being winter it was often accompanied by drizzly rain. In fact that type of weather was often referred to as Fair Mo weather.

My generation was born too late to appreciate Fair Mo. I remember some stannens (stalls) in Gabriel Street outside the Library, also in the Greencourt (Tregenna Place). They sold water pistols and tweeting birds on elastic. They also sold almonds, macaroons and gingerbread nuts. The stannens had large lanterns lit with paraffin. Apart from the extra pocket money the Fair Mo of past years has ceased to exist.

The Fair Mo of 1902 was remembered for its weather

rather than its fairings:

SWS Saturday last was Fair Mo and it was celebrated in swimming style. Of course we had the proverbial wet weather, the rain descended in torrents, a perfect deluge, and continued more or less heavily during the whole of the day.

The year 1920 brought little cheer:

WE The rain, muddy roads and partially lit streets made it of a dull and cheerless nature. There were four stalls in Gabriel Street and most of the shops were kept busy.

Fair Mo in 1924 had a special appeal to the children:

WE Large assortment of toys, games, books etc.

W.H.& A.E.Daggett,

Cash drapery and clothing stores,

50 Fore Street.

In 1927 we were advised to go to Hamlyn's and get the best fairings:

WE Hamlyns fairings are known all over the world and have enjoyed an excellent reputation for nearly a century.

Special gingernuts 1/- per lb.

Best gingernuts 1/6 per lb.

The fact that there was no money in the town because of the failure of the herrings to arrive in 1933 caused Wayfarer in his column to hit the nail on the head:

WE On Saturday it was so cold that all thoughts of Fair Mo had vanished and it was not until midday when a couple of stalls were being erected that I had a reminder.

In the evening, walking through the streets, one noticed the youngsters enjoying themselves with tickling sticks. The streets were full, and a casual glance would leave the impression that Fair Mo was as jolly as ever.

In many homes there were no fairings. The jostling crowd meant a few moments of forgetfulness before going home to wait another opportunity to capture the secret of Fair Mo frivolity, the herring. No fish - no fun. How can we expect families with no income, quite likely a regular weekly loss in its stead, to look as though they were enjoying themselves?

Although the herring were still scarce in 1934 the weather still attracted the headlines:

WE The youngsters engaged in battles with water pistols, not that it mattered a lot, because Fair Mo lived up to its traditional rainy weather and the few drops from water pistols could not be noticed among the millions falling from the sky.

Guise Dancing

The period between Christmas Day and Twelfth Night was devoted to guise dancing. It was the custom for people to go in disguise from house to house, boys dressed as girls and girls dressed as boys, with faces covered with lace and speaking in a high voice. They were received with some apprehension, but given food and drink before moving on somewhere else. No entry was forced and it was all for fun. In other parts of the town more organised things went on. It was more of a fancy dress dance in an attempt to cut out the rough play which had plagued the event over the years, but for Downlong the custom of visiting peoples' homes continued until the outbreak of the war.

SWS January 1900 GUISE DANCING AT ST. IVES by Sampson Taylor Rowe. From all I can gather guise dancing at St. Ives at the best must in itself be but a sorry spectacle, a combination of senseless buffoonism, idiotic posturing, half savage barbarism and offensive exhibitions of the shady side of the human character.

I learn with the greatest satisfaction that the worthy Mayor of St. Ives, Mr. E.Hain, in consideration of the misery and mourning which has fallen upon many a household, arising from the South African war, has prohibited guise dancing at St. Ives for the year 1900.

On Twelfth Night or Epiphany Eve, people parade the principal streets, many dressed up, shouting, singing, dancing, and an indulgence in rough kind of play, which sometimes ends in broken heads, broken glass and belabouring one another with anything handy in the form of a cudgel.

122

SWS January 1901 The old custom of guise dancing at St. Ives has been freely indulged in, dressed in all kinds of fantastic costumes, walking, running, skipping and waltzing through the town to all kinds of music from the modest penny whistle to the more dignified bigotphone bands.

WE January 23rd 1921 GUISE DANCING. The ancient custom has been indulged in during the past fortnight and the young folk have had quite a rollicking time. The costumes have been unique and varied, and the streets have presented an animated appearance. A large number ventured out in disguise on Tuesday, this being the last night for the season.

WE January 14th 1922 GUISE DANCING. The old fashioned custom has been freely engaged in at St. Ives during the past week, the favourable weather adding much to the popularity of the proceedings.

WE 1923 Quite a revival of this old custom has been witnessed in our streets during the past fortnight. Every night scores of youngsters have been parading, dressed in all sorts of gaudy and picturesque costumes, which must have taxed their ingenuity to create. The popularity of this form of innocent merriment is evident by the numbers of people in the thoroughfares each night to watch the proceedings. Tonight (Friday) is the last night for the season.

WE 1925 OLD LOCAL CUSTOM REVIVED by John Citizen.

St. Ives was agog with enthusiasm on Wednesday evening when an organised attempt was made to revive the ancient local custom of guise dancing. Of late years the custom had sadly degenerated and it was felt by many that either something ought to be done to revive guise dancing, or else request the authorities to prohibit it altogether.

The Big Boy's School

Let us return to school life. The time has come to move to the Big Boys next door to the infants. The Headmaster is Mr. W. W. Bastian, a real gentleman, the son of a local fishing family, although at no time did his speech betray his local roots.

With more boys than the school could accommodate, it was necessary for one class to be taught at the Wesley Hall. After Assembly we used to march down the Stennack each morning. During our stay there we sat an examination known as the Scholarship. Those who passed went to Penzance County School. Some went at their parents' expense to Hayle, and the rest of us were together from class to class until we left school at the age of fourteen.

The teachers were all men and worthy of recall. Mr.W.Lawry M.B.E. was much respected. If the maths got a bit difficult it was very easy to get him talking about the fishing. It would appear that as a youth he went to the North Sea fisheries and it took only a chance remark and we were back in Scarborough with our grandfathers, much to the delight of teacher and scholars alike.

It would take a page of its own to talk of Mr.W.J.Sullivan. At election time for the Council we were recruited to parade the town singing the following song, which carried with it the hint of a pasty supper if he were elected :

Vote vote vote for Mr. Sullivan,
He's the man for me and you,
If you vote for him you'll find
That he always speaks his mind
And he does the things you want for him to do-oo-oo.

Jan, as he was affectionately called, was a dab hand with a piece of chalk, both on the blackboard and from the back of the classroom to some unsuspecting misbehaving pupil. In the difficult war years of 1943 and 1944 he was Mayor of the Borough.

If you were musical Mr.L.W.Dunstan would be after you for the School choir. If woodwork was your interest you would be in the carpentry shed in the playground. There Mr.Litt was always sure of attention when he removed and cleaned his glass eye.

Sport did not figure highly in the school curriculum. Rugby and cricket were played in their seasons at the school field at Ayr, and those who were interested in swimming used to be taken for lessons to Porthminster beach, this being the only occasions that Downlong boys ever visited 'Mester beach.

For those with an interest in insect life there was a little white insect that lived in the hole under the inkwell. This was trapped in a circle of ink on top of the desk and remained in the circle until the ink dried. I'm sure many will remember this, although the lessons have long been forgotten.

Everyone went home for dinner, there being no catering facilities at the School. There was a habit then of hanging on to the tail board of lorries for a lift, but this was frowned upon by wiser heads and has now ceased. Another common practice was that if a boy had an apple there would be others asking what he intended to do with the core and they would not be too pleased if the core was well cleaned before being passed over.

Aeroplanes were still a novelty, everyone stopping play to look at any flying overhead. The biggest hindrance to getting to School on time was the steam roller and the tar machine working anywhere in the area, these being of interest to all boys.

WE 1913 Thousands of people turned out at St. Ives on Wednesday morning 27th September to witness an aeroplane flight over St. Ives. The pre-arranged signal to warn St. Ives people of the the Flying Man's approach was a lifeboat rocket. Shortly after 11 o'clock Mr. Gustav Hamel was sighted flying over from Carbis Bay at about 300 feet. He gracefully circled St. Ives where the school children and others gave him a rousing cheer.

The School dentist setting up his chair in the Cookery Department of the Big Girls was a regular dislike, also the visit of Nurse Grey to inspect the ears, eyes and hair. This was the cause of many innocent heads being put through the rigours of the small tooth comb.

One of the highlights of my schooldays was a trip to London. We left on the Friday evening and returned on Sunday morning. The return rail fare, third class, in 1937 was £2.10s.6d. for an adult. Bed and breakfast in Russell Square was advertised at 9s.6d., so altogether we paid about £2.10s. We paid instalments towards this as the total was probably a full week's wage for a man working ashore.

The Union flag was always hoisted on the flagstaff in the garden on Empire Day. There was a large eucalyptus tree in the garden and goldfish in the pond. When we had absorbed all the learning that we could, we spent more time each week weeding the garden area.

WE 1923 At the Boys School Annual Prize Day for the year ending 31st May 1923, perfect attenders were William Warren, 6 years; Peter L.Pearce, 5 years; J.Richards, W.J.Hicks and Ambrose Osborne, 3 years.

WE 1924 At the commencement of the Autumn term of 1924 Mr.C.H.Bray from the National School took over as Headmaster of the Boys School from Mr.H.Harvey, who had been Headmaster at the School for 13 years, having succeeded Mr.T.A.Kay on May 1st 1911. Mr.Bray brought great honour to the School on the sports scene.

In September 1924 the St. Ives Elementary School Swimming Gala was different on two points. The Church authorities had closed the National School, so the old rivalry was missing, and a new spirit of rivalry was introduced by competition swimming under House colours.

WE The boys by ballot had been enrolled as members of one of three houses - 100 yards relay race House representatives:

1. Treloyhan   J.Ellis, T.Ward, N.Bosanquet
2. Trewhella   J.W.Perkin, C.Stevens, J.Woolcock
3. Tregenna   H.Kernick, W.Care
The sculling race was held in two heats:
1st heat   1. J.Murrish 2. J.P.Richards 3. R.Cocking
2nd heat   1. C.B.Noall 2. J.P.Veal 3. W.M.Perkin 4. C.Andrews

January 1925 saw the first officially recognised School rugby match in Cornwall, when, at Higher Tregenna, St. Ives Council School defeated Lescudjack School, Penzance, by 26 points, 1 goal 7 tries to nil. The St. Ives team on this occasion was H.Hawke, E.Gyles, W.Roach (capt), W.J.Hicks, A.Rowe, Job Woolcock, J.Ellis, M.Woolcock, H.Kernick, J.James, J.Tanner, R.Peters, W.G.Care, R.Bennetts, with reserves J.Harry, L.Whitford and E.Woolcock.

The *Sheerness* by the quay. The steam capstan seems to indicate that she is about to load pilchard nets before going to Newlyn to pursue the Mounts Bay fishery.

Deck boards being scrubbed in a convenient pool whilst awaiting a cart to take the herring from the *Bonnie Girls* to be counted. The *Boy Ernest,* arrived too late to reach her mooring, is still unmeshing herring.

St. Ives Herring Fleet – the outside two tiers of boats contain twelve boats often referred to as the big gigs to distinguish them from the clinker sailing and rowing gigs. Each was built to the owner's preference by local boat builders on the harbour sand or in nearby workshops. With the introduction of motors during the 1st World War these boats replaced the former sailing craft with pointed sterns of which five can be seen in the picture. Not only did they draw less water but their colours broke away from the traditional tar with white, blue and green hulls.

Opposite page: The St. Ives rowing/sailing lifeboat *James Stevens No. 10,* after 33 years service at St. Ives, came back as a motor pleasure boat engaged in trips from Porthminster beach. The *Humility,* SS 99, also began life as a sailing boat in 1895 and fished from the port until sold to a buyer in Wales for more fishing in 1943.

The harbour sand and the 'Prom' alive with activity as herrings are being landed. The womenfolk with their wrap-over pinnies and soggets have caught up with the counting and are awaiting another cartload of fish. The boxes and barrels not used during the day will become hiding places when the boys play 'sides' later in the evening. *c1928*.

Opposite page: The smoke vents on the roof of the left hand house shows it to be a Smoke House where herrings were turned into kippers. Formerly Rouncefield's it was owned by Pawlyn before it became a Milk Bar to meet the needs of visitors after the herring fishery declined. The St. Ives pilots had their own boathouse next door to the Copper Kettle cafe with its large copper kettle swinging proudly in the breeze. *c1930*.

This picture, taken before the Shamrock Lodge was built in 1901, clearly shows Hart's blacksmith shop in front of the Primitive Methodist Chapel. Originally on the site of the Chapel it was moved on rollers in 1830 for the Chapel to be built. For many years after its removal the site was still known as Hart's shop.

The One and All Lodge was undermined by the sea in 1931 and collapsed during exceptionally high tides backed by a 60-70mph gale. *c1910.*

The cleaning of dogfish on the harbour sand was an operation which attracted more gulls than people. Dogfish were not eaten locally but were sent away as flake or rock salmon. The Shamrock Lodge built in 1901, protected in this picture by a wooden groin, now snuggles behind a concrete wall built to keep out German invasion forces during World War 2. *c1929.*

Carbis Bay, Payne's Boating Lake & Wishing Well.

No school treat at Carbis Bay Tea Gardens would be complete without a row around the boating lake.

The German field gun on top of the Island which was brought to St. Ives as a trophy of the 1st World War, was taken away for scrap during the 2nd World War. Knowing nothing of what guns did to people this was a popular plaything as well as a background for a snapshot.

The team was so successful that they won the Championship, being presented with the Dennis Lawry Challenge shield and silver medals at the Recreation Ground in the May of that year. Matt Stevens, J.W.Perkin, T.Perkin and A.Perkin also shared the honours. No doubt as a result of this, in February 1926, William Roach was the first Cornish lad to be selected to play for England. This was as Full Back against Wales at Cardiff.

The St. Ives team won the Shield for five consecutive years and produced many County players. One outstanding performance was the scoring of 5 tries by Ben Penberthy in the 15 points to 9 win over Trewirgie School in 1928. Observers noted that Penberthy would have scored more under better playing conditions.

WE November 1928 In the School Notes, written by W.P.Dunn, he mentioned that the hot milk being served out each morning to the boys was much appreciated, but regretted that there were not enough funds to purchase a school wireless set.

WE 1929 A composition on how to improve the School brought forth three suggestions, which might well have been implemented in time for my generation:

1. That each classroom should have gas light.

2. That there should be an oven for warming pasties.

3. That the School have hot water pipes instead of closed stoves.

1931 was the year when the School reached its Jubilee. The school known as the St. Ives Board School opened on the 17th January 1881. The Headmaster Thomas A.Kay opened with 107 boys. A week later 47 other boys joined and the School was full. Mr. Kay was in charge for 30 years and four months. In an effort to hold some sort of occasion 400 letters were sent to old scholars who had attended between 1881 and 1922. Only three subscriptions were received and the proposed celebration was abandoned by Headmaster C.Bray.

A novel idea to interest the boys was thought of by the Headmaster in July, which also gives an indication of the number of model yachts then in the town. The first model yacht regatta for House points was held at Consols pool in July, the boats being classified according to length. Sixty model yachts were brought to school, but the races were held after school hours.

In November 1933 Mr.W.W.Bastian was appointed Headmaster in place of Mr. Bray, and the school never again reached any high peaks on the playing fields.

The Silver Jubilee of King George V in 1935 was commemorated at the Boys, Girls and Infants Schools by the planting of Viburnum Carlesii trees in the school gardens, with the teachers and one scholar from each class adding a shovelful of earth.

In March 1939, Cornwall County Council accepted a tender of £18,919, with £192.12s.6d. for the furniture, for the building of a new school at the Belyars, which was the beginning of the end of the Stennack schools in the form which they had previously been administered. On the 7th June 1940, fifty three children were transferred to the Stennack School from the Island Road School, and the Belyars School opened on Monday 17th June as a mixed school. The Stennack School finally closed its doors as a school on the opening of the new Junior School in September 1984.

A connection with St. Ives, New South Wales, Australia, was made on Empire Day, 24th May 1909, with a commemorative medal for the scholars and an exchange of flags between the two schools. Flags were again exchanged in May 1939, the cost of the flag being £4.13s.7d, with an airmail postage of 12s.0d.

8 THE BEGINNING OF THE END

Wharf Car Park

There were no parking places in St. Ives when we were boys. Motor traffic was increasing every year, and car parking was a continual problem to be discussed at Council meetings.

A fire in property in Pudding Bag Lane, together with compulsory purchase of buildings in the area, made space available for the first car park in St. Ives. The names Pudding Bag Lane and Water Lane have never been used in St. Ives since. The artists lost one of their favourite subjects, the fishermen their lofts and their homes. During the winter months the boys gained a playing place for their trolleys, but a few more families moved Uplong. It was rumoured that houses were to be built on stilts at the top of the park, but this never came about.

*SWS **August 1890** Pudding Bag Lane has been called by that name for 120 years, but the Town Council has now decided to call it Capel Court.*

***WE March 1925** The Highways Committee of the Town Council recommended that the following tolls be charged for the parking of motor cars at the back of Talland Road, top of Skidden Hill, opposite the Council School in the Stennack, and the Wharf Road, namely sixpence for two hours or less, over two hours 1/- each; and the Toll Collector will be asked to collect these tolls on the same terms as other tolls are collected.*

***WE July 1925** The question of the parking of motor cars is a very important one to the business community of a town like St. Ives. In the near future it is quite likely that public authorities will be called upon to provide a place where motor cars may be left unattended.*

Unfortunately at present there is no such convenience available in St. Ives, and unless our local authorities wish to discourage motorists from coming here, some such open space as the West Pier or the Wharf Road should be set aside for the purpose, at least during the summer months.

WE September 1928 NOTES ABOUT TOWN.

I am told by one who should know, that the number of motor cars visiting St. Ives this summer has exceeded all past records. The question of providing a suitable parking place for cars still remains unresolved, and I hear it suggested that the Council might well consider the advisability of using a portion of the Island Meadow field.

WE March 1930 Town Council - The charge for parking cars.

The Committee recommended the Council to advertise for a Toll Collector for the car park in Dove Street. With reference to the charge for parking cars at the Town Yard, Councillor Bryant suggested that the charge be 1/- per day. Alderman Hollow -"We ought not to kill the goose that lays the golden egg - if we charge 1/- we shall not get anyone there".

WE January 1931 With the reduction in the price of petrol and the increase of motor cars since last season, a new car park large enough to stand at least 100 cars is a vital necessity. A site of such dimension is difficult to obtain at St. Ives, but a move must be made in this direction.

WE May 1931 The Committee, having fully considered the question of providing accommodation for the parking of cars, are of the opinion that the only available site at present is from the West Pier to Northcotes Pier, and recommended the Council to consider the erection of a concrete parking raft on pillars for parking approximately 45 cars. It was decided to consider the matter in full Council at an early date.

WE May 1931 The Council in Committee decided not to build a car park on pillars between the West Pier and Northcotes Pier.

WE July 1933 St. Ives Town Council - Demolition of old property.

Counc. Freeman:- "Has the property at Norway been

130

demolished?"

    The Surveyor:- "The work is proceeding."

    Counc. Sullivan then proposed that the Council ask Mr. Ivor Short for a price in respect of the whole of his holdings at Norway Square, Norway Lane, Pudding Bag Lane and Water Lane.

    Counc. Bray:- "I will second that if it is in the mind of the Council to provide a parking place."

    The resolution was carried.

WE Sept 1933 *Urgent need for a car park - Sgt. Hoskin's comments.   Fifteen motorists were summonsed at St. Ives on Wednesday, the majority for causing obstruction by leaving cars unattended. After the cases had been dealt with, Police Sgt. Hoskin referred to the lack of proper parking arrangements for cars, and stated that in addition to the cases brought forward, hundreds of verbal cautions had been issued. He had known motorists to be ordered away during the summer because the West Pier, the only official parking place, was filled with cars.*

WE March 1936 *Passing of Pudding Bag Lane.*

    The hammers of the house-breaker have done their work. It is now a mass of broken stones. In a few months, when visitors flock to St. Ives, cars will be parked there, and the strange name will be forgotten.

To the Hills

The greatest change in the way of life of the Downlong community came in the mid-1930's. No doubt many of the houses were very old, very small and overcrowded. At the slightest excuse property was condemned, in some cases demolished. The start of the war saw many of the houses re-occupied, some by evacuees from London, but a whole section had been removed to make the car park which had been long sought by the Council. This became known as the Sloop car park, which has given much free publicity to an Inn which had no part of it in the park until the removal of the public toilets in 1987.

    People who had lived all their lives with the sea against

their walls, often with only two rooms and perhaps a cellar, found themselves in a strange part of the town which had been farmland, and now had a spare bedroom and a bathroom as well as a garden at the front and back of the house. They had been uprooted from everything they knew and were banished to the outskirts of the town, or "up in the hills" as it was often referred to.

The houses were known officially as the "Ayr Estate", but because of the white exteriors were more popularly known as "China Town" or "The White City". All sorts of good natured rumours spread about people keeping coal in the bath, but this was a big factor in destroying the community life Downlong, as playmates moved with the completion of another block. The sad thing about this exodus was that many of the Downlong houses are still standing, and with the return of the evacuees and the arrival of people with more money than many fishermen had ever seen, the houses were bought and modernised as second homes or business ventures, so making Downlong a ghost town for the greater part of the year.

WE *June 1919* *Town Council - Housing scheme.*

The Mayor thought St. Ives proportion would be 140 houses, proposed site westward from Bullans Lane hill to the small wooden gate at Ayr leading to St. Johns Church.

Counc. Daniel did not think any fisherman could afford £20 a year rent.

Ald. Daniel - the rents in the lower part of the town varied from £4 to £8 per year.

WE *Feb 1920* *Town Council - Housing problem.*

The Housing Committee instructed the Surveyor to prepare a scheme for the erection of approximately 60 houses at Cemetery Field and the Island Meadow, with an alternative scheme for the same number of houses at Ayr.

WE *March 1920* *Town Council.*

The Mayor read the report of the Housing Committee to build 116 houses on the approved site at Ayr and west of Bullans Lane.

The building line will be varied and broken; the design

of the houses varied and harmonious; the long uninteresting terrace type being eliminated. Here and there will be green patches, a crescent or two, groups of shrubs and trees.

WE March 1921 *Council new plan for houses on Island Meadow.*

At the monthly meeting of the St. Ives Town Council it was recommended that the Bullans Lane housing scheme be abandoned and that the Ministry be asked to approve a scheme for the erection of houses on the Island Meadow.

WE December 1924 *Council meeting - working class houses needed.*

Counc. Bray called attention to the need of providing real working class houses, especially for the fishermen, whose dwellings should be adjacent to their work. Some of the fishermen were living as far up as Nanjivey. Counc. Toy mentioned that workmen in the lower parts of the town had been squeezed out by the artists.

WE January 1927 *New housing scheme.*

After several delays and disappointments in regard to the provision of additional housing accommodation, it seems that the St. Ives Town Council have at last definitely made up their minds to go ahead with a scheme. Counc. Hunkin opposed the scheme, remarking that according to official figures 140 houses had been built in St. Ives during the past five years, and since the last census the population had declined by 600.

The Bullans Lane layout of 34 houses, two blocks of 8 houses in a terrace and two of 9 was accepted.

WE May 1927 *Borough of St. Ives.*

The St. Ives Town Council, as the first stage of their proposed housing scheme, contemplate erecting 16 dwelling houses, containing three bedrooms, sitting room, kitchen, scullery and bathroom, which can be let at a rental of £24 per annum exclusive of rates.

Applications for renting to be delivered in writing at the office of the undersigned by 12 noon Friday May 13th inst. T.J.Chellew, Town Clerk

WE May 1927 St. Ives housing scheme.

The Town Councillors of St. Ives were confronted with a difficult problem on Monday, when they were called upon to make a definite decision in regard to the Bullans Hill housing scheme, and eventually they decided on a further postponement, thus endangering their right of receiving the government subsidy of £9 per house.

The Town Clerk said 13 applications had been received, but the people who lived in the congested district could not afford to pay £24 per year. Only four applicants were from people living below the Market House and two were from persons living out of town, but employed at Crysede works.

WE May 1927 Difficulty in naming new council houses.

Suggestion that it be called Pendennis Terrace turned down as it had a Falmouth atmosphere. Counc. Bray replied that the Committee found that all the St. Ives names had already been used up. One member hazarded Clifton Terrace as it was near a cliff, and Counc. Prynne said: "Call it Hard Climb Terrace and you won't be far off the mark". Eventually referred to Committee.

WE June 1927 Name of new council houses.

In a book of Cornish names it was found that Bos Stennack means "dwellings in the Stennack". It was agreed that the new houses be known as Bostennack Terrace.

WE December 1927 Notes about Town.

The walls of the council houses are beginning to be visible from the road. There is no doubt that they will be some of the nicest little houses in St. Ives. Being double-fronted the whole house is conveniently arranged and there will be a minimum of work for mothers. Large windows will make the houses very light, and consequently very healthy, for there is no disputing that sunlight exercises a very beneficial effect on health.

There are only eight houses to be built, but one hopes that others may be erected later for the many who are in need.

WE March 1928 *St. Ives Town Council.*

Applications were considered for renting the eight council houses now in the course of construction, and it was decided to recommend the following:-
Mrs.J.Barnes, Mr.L.C.Harvey, Mr.J.N.Bennetts, Mrs.M.Kemp, Mrs.L.Burt, Mr.S.H.Stevens, Mr.L.B.Cogan, Mr.L.Styles
As weekly tenants at a rental of 8s.6d a house, exclusive of rates.

WE Feb 1929 *Housing needs of St. Ives. Three schemes to be considered.*

Ald. Beckerleg thought they should build on the Island Meadow, the fishermen needed houses and they should be erected near the mens' calling. The Mayor stated that according to an agreement, the Council would have to pay £200 to the representatives of the Cowley Estate before they could build on the Island. Eventually it was decided to prepare estimates for three schemes, viz. the Recreation Ground site, Island Meadow and parallel with Alexandra Terrace.

WE April 1929 *Recreation Ground site turned down. Agreed, a scheme for building 20 houses fronting west on land to the rear of Alexandra Terrace*

WE May 1931 *Council housing.*

The Committee recommended the Council to invite tenders for the erection of 8 non-parlour type houses with bay windows, in two blocks of four, at Ayr, and 7 non-parlour type houses, without bay windows, at Bostennack Terrace.

A petition received from 47 residents at Ayr: "To erect council houses in the immediate vicinity will be a grave injustice to present property owners by seriously depreciating values".

WE October 1931 *Council housing.*

The Committee recommended that the council houses recently erected at Ayr be known as Alexandra Place.

Counc. Sullivan said the tenants themselves had started to call the place Alexandra Place, and seeing they had adopted that name the Committee accepted it.

WE May 1932 *Rents of council houses.*

The rents of the Ayr houses be 3/- per week plus rates.

2,3,5 and 6 Bostennack be 3/3 per week plus rates.

1 and 7 Bostennack be 3/6 per week plus rates.

4 Bostennack be 3/9 per week plus rates.

WE Dec 1933 *The housing tenders.*

The tender of £3,660 from Mr.W.Fairbrother had been accepted for 12 houses at Bullans Lane.

WE Feb 1936 *Five houses to be erected in Virgin Street.*

EPILOGUE

Although the decline in local fishing and the removal of its people to the Council housing estate at Ayr played a big part, the outbreak of World War Two was another blow to the way of life that had existed in Downlong for many years. Although the scenes of World War One, when the fishermen of the Royal Naval Reserve marched to the railway station in their hundreds were not repeated, there was still a big exodus of men. In addition to those in the Services, coach loads of men left every day to work on airfield construction at Mullion and other places. Men not likewise engaged were busy making camouflage nets, either in the Island factory or at home, a job which entailed long hours with scant reward.

With the end of the war, returning men found boats, nets and gear which had deteriorated over the years, other men were no longer able to work owing to war injuries, and still more had not returned for a variety of reasons, all adding to the drain on the fishing community.

The destruction of Downlong commenced with the sale of the first "Fisherman's Cottage" to come up at auction. The astounding price paid for one house was equal to what a whole row had been built for. It was said that the money had been earned on war work with people working long hours. Whatever they had been making, it certainly wasn't camouflage nets, but where the damage was caused was the fact that the local people could not compete.

As house after house came on the market every street and row was affected and the whole of Downlong was turned into a ghost town for eight months of the year as properties were turned into holiday accommodation by absent landlords for the four months of the year which are ironically known as "the season".

A community can only exist where there are people that live together, know and help each other. Now, neighbours come for a week or a fortnight, and are gone for ever. Steps and gutters which were scrubbed every Friday evening or Saturday morning, now never see a broom. Windows that were "skeeted" every week now only get wet when it rains. Where doors used to slam and feet used to run before the smoke of the lifeboat maroon left the sky, regardless of time of day or night, there is now no reaction.

People die and are buried, without a neighbouring blind being drawn, often because they don't know of the death, and this in a part of the town where everyone was related. The ringing of the Town Crier's bell used to warn of the water being turned off or a sale by public auction, now, if the harbour was sold it wouldn't cause a ripple.

In common with every other place all doors are locked, and this in an area where doors were never locked, especially during the herring season when men came and went at all hours of the night.

The policeman was known by name, and everyone spoke to him as he walked around his beat across the harbour front. The doctors were familiar figures as they did their rounds of the sick.

The 1974 re-organisation of the Councils also had its effect. No longer could one go the Guildhall and explain things to the Surveyor. It's now a telephone call to an unknown at Penzance, which to many is not worth the hassle. We are now a part of Penwith, a name which has no significance Downlong, and is not even pronounced the same as in the old Penwith area, in some cases PENwith, others PenWITH.

With the widely held view of the older generation that "our little town has been destroyed" no part of the town has suffered more than the lower part. The fishing industry in St. Ives had many allied industries situated Downlong: boatbuilders, fish cellars, smoke houses, basket makers, net lofts, buyers, marine engineers, blacksmiths, haulage firms and a public weighbridge, all employing men, but apart from a few net lofts nothing is left.

With the scarcity of fish and the change of the town to cater only for the holiday industry, it was inevitable that

138

new uses would have to be found for the buildings that were previously dependent on fish. That these places should be open only in the summer season, because of the type of business engaged in, helps to spread the feeling of desolation for the rest of the year.

The local elections used to be a time of interest, although the candidate might not be a "hake" at least he was known to everyone. Now there are no local, district or county councillors living Downlong. In a recent election one candidate boasted that he lived in the ward, but this was a mile above the Market House.

A survey carried out in the Spring of 1987 shows some revealing facts. Of the 24 houses in Carncrows Street only 12 were occupied by just 18 people. Of the 19 houses in St. Peters Street only 3 were occupied by 5 people and every street in Downlong shows the same situation. This in an area where every house used to be occupied all the year round, often by large families. Every street had a "character" of some repute. Now there are no characters worth writing about. Very few people for most of the time, and the old way of life gone for ever.

That such great changes could be possible in sixty years is almost unbelievable. I therefore thank God for every remembrance of those who over the years have studied at the Breakwater College, have dried their washing on the Island slopes, stayed out over the low water, tacked across 'Meor, or just sat on Dobles Wall, because many of us believe there is still no spot in all the world quite like it.

GLOSSARY

Balsh	Rope
Barwell	Waterproof apron
Bay man	Man from Mounts Bay
Billis	Fire bellows
Boot jack	Wooden sea boot remover
Cherks	Partly burnt coal
Creaved	Partly cooked pastry
Dicks Hill	Now Fish Street
Dumble dory	June bug
Emmets	Ants
Epps	Door cut in half horizontally (stable door)
Flambeau	Paraffin soaked flare
Flasket	A basket, mostly for carrying washing
Flies	Hands of a clock
Frail	Canvas bag
Grace	Grease
Grammersows	Wood lice
Grushens	Dregs at the bottom of a tea cup
Gurry	Wooden box with shafts for carrying herring
Gwenders	Frostbite
Jan Dark	Mystical figure about at night
Kidda	Guillemot
Launders	Roof gutters
Maw	Slice of bread
Mollick	Canvas float
Mulley	Rock pool fish
Norman	Winkle
Planchon	Floor board
Policeman gull	Black backed gull
Raw fry	Fried meal of potato, cabbage etc.
Rep	A box for tackle
Riffle	Slipped slates on a roof
Schale	Fish scale
Shang	Broken net mesh
Skeeter	Brass pump for washing windows
Slab	Coal fired cooking range
Soggett	Hessian apron
Tommy Tribes Bay	Untidy room
Whistle fish	Rock pool fish
Wilk	Stye on the eye
Wink	A frame for net cotton
Wisht	Poorly looking

FAMILY TREE (part)

My Father's side

Thomas Rowe m. Johanna Davies

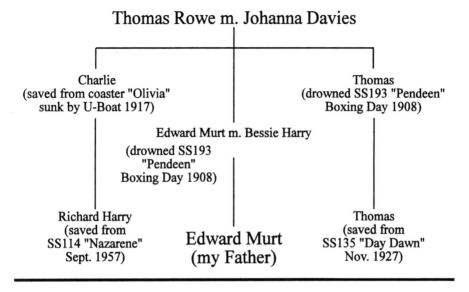

Charlie
(saved from coaster "Olivia"
sunk by U-Boat 1917)

Thomas
(drowned SS193 "Pendeen"
Boxing Day 1908)

Edward Murt m. Bessie Harry
(drowned SS193
"Pendeen"
Boxing Day 1908)

Richard Harry
(saved from
SS114 "Nazarene"
Sept. 1957)

**Edward Murt
(my Father)**

Thomas
(saved from
SS135 "Day Dawn"
Nov. 1927)

My Mother's side

William Eddy m. Eliza Richards

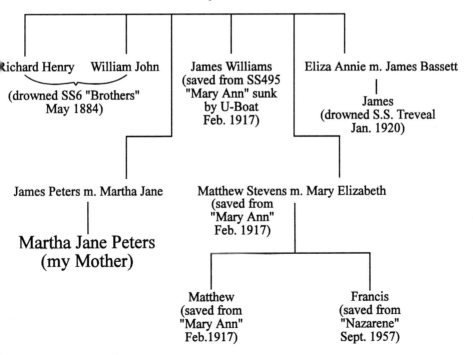

Richard Henry   William John
(drowned SS6 "Brothers"
May 1884)

James Williams
(saved from SS495
"Mary Ann" sunk
by U-Boat
Feb. 1917)

Eliza Annie m. James Bassett
James
(drowned S.S. Treveal
Jan. 1920)

James Peters m. Martha Jane

Matthew Stevens m. Mary Elizabeth
(saved from
"Mary Ann"
Feb. 1917)

**Martha Jane Peters
(my Mother)**

Matthew
(saved from
"Mary Ann"
Feb.1917)

Francis
(saved from
"Nazarene"
Sept. 1957)